Dear Reading Detective,

Welcome to Kingdom Files! You're now a very important part of the Kingdom Files investigation—a series of really cool biographies all found in the Bible. Each case you investigate focuses on an important Bible character and is separated into three sections to make your time fun and interesting. First, you'll find the **Fact File**, which contains key information about a specific Bible character whom God called to do big things for His kingdom. Next, you'll read through an **Action File** that lays out Bible events showing the character in action. And finally, the **Power File** is where you'll find valuable information and memory verses to help you see how God is working in your life too. Along the way, **Clue Boxes** will offer applications to help you keep track of your thoughts as you make your way through the files. You can also use these sections to record questions you might have along David's journey. Write down any questions, and then ask your parents to get them involved in your quest.

Before you begin, know this: not only did God have plans for the Bible characters you'll read about in the Kingdom Files, but Jeremiah 29:11 says that God has big plans for you too! I pray that *Kingdom Files: Who Was David?* helps you get a bigger picture of God and that you will see just how much He loves you!

Blessings,

M.K.

Name: **DAVID**

Occupation: **king, mighty warrior, writer of psalms**

From: **Bethlehem**

Years Active: **1025–970 BC**

Kingdom Work: **king of Israel, fought for God's people, wrote songs**

Mini Timeline:

1025 BC
Samuel anoints David as future king

1020 BC
David kills Goliath

993 BC
David reigns over all Israel and Judah

The Kingdom Files

The Kingdom Files
Complete 6-Story Collection

Matt Koceich

BARBOUR **kidz**
A Division of Barbour Publishing

Cover illustration by C. B. Canga.
Interior illustrations by Patricia Yuste, Jon Davis, and Eva Morales.

Published by Barbour Publishing, Inc., 1810 Barbour Drive, Uhrichsville, Ohio 44683, www.barbourbooks.com

Our mission is to inspire the world with the life-changing message of the Bible.

Member of the
Evangelical Christian
Publishers Association

Printed in the United States of America.
001233   0422   BP

Kingdom Files:
Who Was David?

Key Stats:

- ✦ Brought the people of Israel together
- ✦ Helped the Israelites win battles and conquer land
- ✦ Made it possible for his son Solomon to build the temple

 CLUES

The temple was built in Jerusalem and was mainly used as the place to offer sacrifices to God. The most important part of the temple was called the holy of holies, and in it were the Ten Commandments and the ark of the covenant. Once a year, the high priest would go into the holy of holies, pray to God, and ask God to forgive the people of Israel's sins.

Early Life

To begin our investigation into the life of David, it helps to understand a few background notes first. David's story is found in the Old Testament books of 1 Samuel, 2 Samuel, 1 Kings, and 1 Chronicles. When David was young, a king named Saul had ruled over the land of Israel for forty-two years. He became selfish, so God decided to call a new young man to take the throne.

God sent his prophet, Samuel, to David's house. So Samuel went to Bethlehem where he found a man named Jesse, who was David's father. David was the youngest of eight sons. He worked as a shepherd tending his father's

flock. Jesse introduced his sons to Samuel, but the prophet asked if there were any others. That's when Jesse called for David, and immediately Samuel knew this was who he was supposed to anoint as king. The Bible says that at this point, the Spirit of God came on David with power (1 Samuel 16:13).

Meanwhile, King Saul was being attacked by an evil spirit. He asked his servants to bring someone who could play music to help calm his

nerves. The servants knew about David, and so Jesse sent his son David to Saul with a donkey loaded with bread and wine and a young goat as gifts for the king. Saul was so pleased with David and his music playing that he had David stay with him to be in his service.

At the same time, there was an army called the Philistines who were close by, trying to attack the Israelites. King Saul gathered the Israelites to fight and defend their towns (1 Samuel 17:2–3). When they went out to engage in battle, Saul and his men were confronted by a horrifying sight. There was one Philistine in particular named Goliath. The Bible says that Goliath was over nine feet tall and wore a bronze helmet and armor that

 CLUES

Even the giant's spear had a fifteen-pound iron point!

weighed 125 pounds!

The giant began taunting the king and his army. Goliath yelled out a challenge. He asked for a man who would be willing to fight him. He said that if he won, the Israelites would become slaves to the Philistines; and if one of Saul's men won, the Philistines would become servants to the Israelites. King Saul was terrified! (1 Samuel 17:11).

This exchange went on for forty days. Morning and night, Goliath approached the Israelites, asking for a man who would be willing to fight. No one dared fight the superhuman giant.

Meanwhile, David was in charge of taking food to his older brothers. They were a part of the Israelite army and within clear view of the giant. David ran out to the battle lines to check on his brothers and make sure they were okay. As soon as David saw Goliath, he wanted to know who

CLUES

David told Saul about how when lions or bears would come to capture the sheep, he would go after the predators and save the sheep from being eaten. He also added that if the animal tried to attack him, he was strong enough to take its life. David then compared Goliath to the wild animals: "The LORD who rescued me from the paw of the lion and the paw of the bear will rescue me from the hand of this Philistine" (1 Samuel 17:37).

he was. David was upset because of the way the giant didn't respect God (1 Samuel 17:26).

David's oldest brother was angry at him, because he thought David was only there to watch a good fight. Saul heard about David's courage and sent for him. In the king's chambers, David told Saul not to lose heart because of Goliath's threats. And then David offered to go and fight the giant!

Saul wasn't convinced. He thought David was too young and unable to win a battle with the giant. Saul added that Goliath had been a warrior for a very long time. But David was ready with a reply. He told Saul about his job tending sheep.

King Saul finally agreed to let David go and fight the giant. He began by putting his personal armor on David. But David couldn't move around in the heavy armor. David armed himself with only his staff and his sling, and he chose five stones from a nearby stream and put them in a pouch. Then he went out to meet Goliath.

The superhuman laughed. "Am I a dog, that you come at me with sticks? . . . Come here. . .and I'll give your flesh to the birds and the wild animals!" (1 Samuel 17:43–44). David knew that God was on his side and responded to the giant not with fear but with courage. "You come against me with sword and spear and javelin, but I come against you in the name of the LORD Almighty"

(1 Samuel 17:45). David said that he was confident that God would deliver the giant into his hands. And then he added that after he won the battle, the  whole world would know that God was in charge.

David also said that the battle belonged to God and that God would give not only Goliath but all the Philistines into the Israelites' hands. At that, the giant moved quickly to attack David. David didn't hesitate. He ran toward the giant. As he ran, David took a stone and slung it at Goliath. The stone hit the giant on the forehead, causing him to fall dead "facedown on the ground" (1 Samuel 17:49). At the sight of this unbelievable event, the Philistines took off running. David kept Goliath's weapons. King Saul was very impressed that David had taken care of the wicked giant and a very massive problem!

In the King's Service

Saul kept David with him instead of letting him return home to Bethlehem. A man named Jonathan, who was the king's eldest son, befriended David during this time. Saul sent David on many missions. David was very successful and was given a high rank in the king's army. All  the troops were grateful for David's promotion.

The Bible says that one day when David was playing music, an evil spirit came over Saul and he tried to throw a spear at David, but David

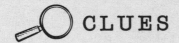

CLUES

Soon the people were praising David more than they were praising King Saul—and this made the king angry. He kept a close watch on David to make sure he didn't take more attention from the king.

was quick to move out of the way. Saul soon became afraid of David. He put David in charge of a thousand men to lead into battles. David had success in everything he did because "the LORD was with him" (1 Samuel 18:14). The Israelite people continued to love David because of his great leadership.

Saul became very worried that David would take his throne, so he tried to trick the young man. He wanted David to marry his older daughter, but David didn't feel worthy, so the marriage never happened. But Saul wouldn't take no for an answer. He offered his other daughter's hand in marriage. Saul had his

attendants talk to David to try to convince him to agree to the union. But again, David said he wasn't worthy of marrying the king's daughter because he was "a poor man and little known" (1 Samuel 18:23).

Saul couldn't believe David's refusal, because he wanted David to obey him. The king tried sending David back out to battle, hoping that the Philistines would take his life. But nothing went the way Saul wanted it to go. David eventually married Saul's daughter, and Saul realized that the Lord was with David. The Bible says that Saul "remained his enemy the rest of his days" (1 Samuel 18:29).

CLUES

The king's plan continued to backfire. The more David battled the Philistines, the more success he had. As a result, David became more and more popular among the people. So Saul stopped trying to come up with different ways to hurt David. His new plan? He ordered his son Jonathan and all the servants to take David's life.

Since Jonathan was David's friend, he told him of his father's plan to take his life. Jonathan told David to hide and also said that he would talk to Saul in hopes of helping David. Jonathan told his father that David was a good person and that David hadn't done anything wrong. In fact, he said everything David had done actually helped Saul.

The king heard his son and came to his senses. He promised he wouldn't do anything to harm David.

But as time passed, once again Saul tried to harm David with a spear. And yet again, David was quicker and avoided getting hurt. After this incident, David escaped the castle. Saul was furious and sent men to David's house in Bethlehem, but David's wife Michal warned him of her father's plan. After David ran away, Michal

took a statue and put it in David's bed. She also covered the idol with some clothes and even put "goats' hair at the head" (1 Samuel 19:13).

The king sent men to capture David, but Michal intercepted them and said that David was sick. Saul wouldn't be defeated and sent his men again to bring David, sick or not, back to him. That's when the men found the statue instead of David. Saul asked his daughter why she had deceived him. She said that David threatened her, even though it had been her idea to help him escape.

Meanwhile, when David fled, he found Samuel and told him everything that had happened with Saul. Then the two of them went to a town called Naioth, about five miles northwest of Jerusalem. Not

 **CLUES**

A prophet was a person chosen by God to speak for Him. They would tell people about God and what He expected, and they would remind people to obey God and to worship Him with all their hearts. Saul's men were overcome by God's Spirit, and they too began praising God along with the prophets.

long after, the king learned where David was and sent men to capture him. The Bible says that when Saul's men arrived at the place where David was staying, they saw Samuel leading a group of prophets prophesying (1 Samuel 19:20).

Saul heard of this and sent more men, but like the first group, they also joined in with the others and began praising God. Saul sent a third group of men, and they also joined the others and praised God. Saul decided to go to find David himself!

When he arrived, the king asked where Samuel and David were and was told to go to Naioth. Then the Spirit came over Saul, and he walked along praising God on his way to find David. He found Samuel and kept prophesying all that day and all through the night. This wasn't what the king had in mind when he went after David. The people were so amazed, they thought Saul was one of the prophets!

3

On the Run

David received word that Saul was after him, so he went back to find his friend Jonathan. Once the two friends were reunited, David asked why Jonathan's father was trying to take his life. Jonathan told David not to worry. He said that his father always told him his plans and that he hadn't heard about the horrible things David was saying.

David told Jonathan that Saul knew he and Jonathan were friends. Saul, in David's opinion, didn't want to see his son grieved by David's passing. But David believed that Saul would still find him and take his life. Jonathan replied, "Whatever you want me to do, I'll do it for you."

Jonathan vowed never to turn David over to his father.

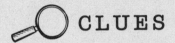

CLUES

David came up with a plan to test the king's heart. He told Jonathan that he was going to hide out in the field. He said that if Saul acted like he missed David, then Jonathan should say that David had gone back to Bethlehem to join his family in an annual sacrifice. David told his friend that if Saul was okay with that, then David knew he was safe. However, David knew that if Saul lost his temper over the story, then he would face extreme danger.

The two friends went out into the fields and came up with an idea. Jonathan told David to hide behind a big stone. He said he would shoot three arrows at it like he was taking target practice. Then when he sent a servant to retrieve the arrows, Jonathan would send David a code so he would know whether it was safe to stay or if he should run away.

The next day when Saul sat with his family for a feast, he noticed that David was absent. Saul

thought nothing of it, but when David was missing from the gathering for the second day's meal, the king asked his son Jonathan for an explanation. Jonathan protected David by telling Saul a story about David's family wanting him there for a sacrifice and that one of David's brothers had ordered him to be there in Bethlehem for it (1 Samuel 20:29).

Saul became infuriated with Jonathan's response because David got away. Saul was angry because he knew that Jonathan had helped David escape. Saul threatened his own son by saying,

CLUES

Jonathan knew that his father intended to kill David. This made Jonathan very sad. He couldn't eat and was very angry and ashamed at the way Saul wanted to mistreat David.

"As long as the son of Jesse lives on this earth, neither you nor your kingdom will be established" (1 Samuel 20:31). Then Saul ordered his son to have

someone find David and bring him to the royal palace. Jonathan tried sticking up for his friend by asking Saul what David had done wrong.

The next morning, Jonathan went out to meet David in the fields. A small boy was with him to collect the arrows. Jonathan yelled out, "Isn't the arrow beyond you? . . . Hurry! Go quickly! Don't stop!" (1 Samuel 20:37–38). This, of course, was the friends' code, and the boy had no idea that David was close by and could hear Jonathan's secret message. When the boy returned the arrows, Jonathan told him to take them back to the village. After the boy left, David came out from his hiding place behind the stone and bowed before Jonathan.

Both men cried together because of the sad news that Saul had every intention of killing David. Finally, Jonathan told David to head out in peace and reminded him that they would be friends forever. Eventually, David left, and Jonathan headed back to town.

The Bible says that David went to a town called Nob where he met the priest Ahimelek. The priest asked David why he was traveling alone. David replied by saying that the king had sent him on a secret mission and that his men were sent in a different direction. David then asked the man for food.

While this was going on, the chief shepherd of Saul was there. David asked the priest if he had a weapon he could borrow. Ahimelek said the sword of Goliath was there. David agreed that it was a special sword, so he took it and fled from

Saul's servant. David went to the king of Gath, Achish. The Bible says that David was afraid of the king and pretended to be insane. David acted like a madman, "making marks on the doors of the gate and letting saliva run down his beard" (1 Samuel 21:13). Achish was enraged. He couldn't believe his servants would bring such a lunatic into his presence.

David took off from Gath and ran to the cave of Adullam. His family received word where David was, and they went to him there.

Soon nearly four hundred men—people who were unhappy, in debt, or stressed out—gathered with

David and "he became their commander" (1 Samuel 22:2).

David continued his escape journey and went to a place called Mizpah in the land of Moab. He found the king in Moab and asked if his parents could stay with him until he learned what God was going to do.

A prophet named Gad came to David and warned him to leave. "Do not stay. . . . Go into the land of Judah" (1 Samuel 22:5). Again, David ran away and headed into the forest of Hereth.

Saul received news that his men had discovered David's whereabouts. He sat holding a spear and addressed all his officials who were nearby. Saul started asking them questions about David's character and intentions. "Will the son of Jesse give all of you fields and vineyards? Will he make all of you commanders of thousands?" (1 Samuel 22:7).

 **CLUES**

Saul was mad because he wanted to know why his men weren't helping him capture David. Saul thought maybe they had made bargains with the fugitive.

One of the king's servants, Doeg the Edomite, spoke up and told Saul about how David went to the man named Ahimelek at Nob and how the man provided for David and even gave him Goliath's sword. This information made Saul angry. The king sent for Ahimelek and questioned him as to why he would help David. The man said

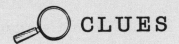

CLUES

Edom was a land that bordered Israel and is now southwest Jordan. It was a popular place because of its location on the trade route between Arabia and the Mediterranean Sea.

that he knew that David was the most loyal servant in all of Saul's army.

Saul ignored the truth and became enraged. He threatened to take the man's life and ordered his guards to take the lives of all the priests because Saul thought they too had helped David. Saul was in for a surprise. His guards refused to obey him. Because they were God's priests, the guards didn't want to harm them.

Saul wouldn't be outdone. He turned to Doeg again and ordered him to strike down the priests. Unlike the guards, Doeg obeyed the command. As Doeg carried out the evil order, one man named Abiathar escaped and found David. He told David of the horrible attack on the priests. David had remorse because he had met Doeg before and had a feeling that he would tell Saul about David and how Ahimelek had helped him. And he felt like he was responsible for the horrible murders. David invited Abiathar to stay with him since they had a common enemy in Saul.

Still Running

A battle was raging near David's location in a place called Keilah. The Philistines were attacking the people and stealing their possessions. David asked God if he should go and attack the Philistines. God said yes and instructed David to save the city. David told his men about the plan, but they were afraid to go into battle against the Philistines. This made David go back to the Lord and ask what he should do. God said, "Go down to Keilah, for I am going to give the Philistines into your hand" (1 Samuel 23:4).

David took his men and went down to Keilah, and they were victorious over the Philistines, saving the people there. Yet again, Saul would not go away or be defeated by David. Saul received information that

David had gone to the town of Keilah.

But this time it was David who received information about Saul's intent to come and attack David. David went to God in prayer, asking if Saul was on his way to attack and if the people of Keilah

CLUES

The king was happy because he felt that David would be easy to capture since he had gone into a town with "gates and bars" (1 Samuel 23:7), meaning it was built up to protect the people who lived there. Saul gathered all his forces to help capture David and his men.

would turn David over to Saul. God answered yes to both questions.

David gathered his men, now totaling around six hundred, and took off in escape. They didn't stop but kept moving from place to place, trying to outwit Saul and his army. Saul was told of David's escape and decided not to go to Keilah. David stayed in the wilderness and in the hills trying to outrun Saul. Saul did try to hunt David down, but he failed because "God did

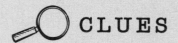 CLUES

At this time, Jonathan, King Saul's son and David's friend, came back into David's life. He found David in Horesh and helped him reconnect with God. Jonathan reminded David to find all his strength in God alone. He said, "Don't be afraid. . . . My father Saul will not lay a hand on you. You will be king over Israel. . . . Even my father Saul knows this" (1 Samuel 23:17). These words helped David know that God was on his side. Jonathan went home, and David remained in Horesh.

not give David into his hands" (1 Samuel 23:14).

Just like all the other times before, while David was being reminded that he was doing God's work, Saul was close on his heels. This time a group of people known as the Ziphites met Saul and told him that they knew exactly where David was hiding. They invited Saul to come down to where they were and offered to hand David over to him. Saul was excited and grateful that someone was willing to help him capture David. Saul told them to get more information, like places David normally went and who went to see him. The king knew David was clever, and he didn't want to lose

CLUES

David and his men were in a place called the Desert of Maon. As Saul and his people gave chase, David was warned about it, so he stayed in the desert. Saul got news of where David was hiding, so he headed to the desert too.

him. Saul wanted definite information about all the hiding places David used. Saul would then be armed with enough information to go after his prey.

In between Saul and David was a large mountain. David and his men were on one side, and Saul and his guards were on the other. Saul was closing the gap. The chase was almost over. Just as Saul and his men were about to capture David, a messenger told Saul that the dreaded Philistines were

raiding the land. When he received this news, Saul broke off from pursuing David and

went out to meet the
Philistines.

After Saul left,
David went and
lived in a place
called En Gedi. Saul
came back from his

CLUES

Crags of the Wild Goats is located in the Judean wilderness. It's made up of rocky cliffs. The ibex mountain goat is found in this area.

pursuit of the Philistines and began to look for
David again. He was given information that David
was staying in a place called the Crags of the Wild
Goats. Saul took three thousand men and went

out in search of
David. Along the
way, Saul entered
a cave, but what
the king didn't
know was that
David and his
men were in the

back of the very same cave. David crept up and cut off a piece of Saul's robe.

David felt bad for what he had done, and he told his men that they were not allowed to attack Saul. They let him leave the cave untouched. After Saul left the cave, David walked out and called out to him, "My lord the king!" (1 Samuel 24:8). Saul turned, and David bowed down. He asked Saul why he had listened to the people who told him that David was trying to harm him. He went on to remind Saul that the Lord had delivered the king into David's hands. He said he had men who had urged him to take Saul's life,  but he refused. David told Saul that he would not harm him and showed him the piece of robe that he had cut off. David was using that as proof that he did not have any intention of harming Saul.

Saul began to cry because he realized that David had spared his life. Saul even asked God to reward David for the way he treated Saul. Saul asked David to promise that he wouldn't harm his family, and David promised. Eventually, Saul returned home, and David and his men returned to their hiding place.

The next part of David's journey took him to Maon, in the area of Carmel. A man named Nabal who was very wealthy lived there. Nabal's wife was Abigail. Nabal owned three thousand sheep, and David heard about him and sent men to him with a message. Nabal had shepherds who had spent time with David's group. David's men had helped protect their flocks. So David sent a message to Nabal in hopes of getting help with food and provisions.

When Nabal listened to David's men, he didn't respond kindly. He questioned who David was and asked why he should share his food with people he didn't know. When David's men returned to him with Nabal's reply, David told them to get their swords. About four hundred men went with David to confront Nabal.

One of Abigail's servants told her that Nabal had hurled insults at David's men earlier in the day. The servant confirmed that David's people had been very good to them and explained how David and his men had protected them while they were out in the fields with the sheep. The servant told Abigail that disaster was on its way because Nabal had dismissed David's plea for help.

Abigail came up with a plan. She gathered up "two hundred loaves of bread, two skins of wine, five dressed sheep, [sixty pounds] of roasted grain, a hundred cakes of raisins, and two hundred cakes of pressed figs" (1 Samuel 25:18). She had it loaded up on donkeys and told her servants to head toward David and his men and that she would follow behind. Abigail did not tell her husband what she was doing. As she rode her donkey, Abigail looked out and saw David and his men approaching in the distance.

Abigail got off her donkey and bowed before David. She asked permission to speak to David, and he listened. Abigail told David not to listen to anything Nabal said. She even told David that her

husband's name meant "fool." Abigail let David know she hadn't seen the group of men he sent who had asked for help. Then she presented the generous food offering to David.

Abigail said that she believed God would be with David, because David fought the Lord's battles. She told him not to worry about being hunted by Saul, because she knew God would protect him. Abigail also told David that she believed he would become the ruler over Israel. She finally asked David to remember her.

When she arrived home, she found that Nabal was having a wild party with a lot of food and drink. The next morning, she told her husband all that had happened with David, and the Bible says Nabal's heart began to hurt. Several days later, Nabal passed away. After

CLUES

David praised God for Abigail. He asked for her to be blessed because of her good judgment and the way her actions helped keep David from attacking Nabal and his men. David accepted Abigail's offering and sent her back home in peace.

word of Nabal's passing reached David, David sent a message back to Abigail asking for her hand in marriage. Abigail agreed and soon became David's wife.

5

So Close

Yet again, Saul went in search of David. The Ziphites told Saul that David was hiding in the hills of Hakilah. Saul gathered three thousand select troops to search for the runaway shepherd. He made a camp by the roadside, but David stayed in the wilderness. David sent scouts to watch Saul, and after a while he went to the place where Saul was. He found where Saul slept and saw his army surrounding him.

David asked his people who would go with him to Saul, and a man named Abishai volunteered. David and his friend went to Saul's camp and found the king sleeping with his spear on the ground nearby. Abishai told David that God had delivered Saul into his hands. He wanted to

be done
with Saul,
but David
warned
against
bringing
harm to
the man,

no matter how bad he was. David knew that
God had anointed Saul, and so David wanted to
respect that fact. David wanted to let God deal
with Saul instead. David made sure they took
Saul's spear and
water jug before
they left his tent.

David crossed
over to the other
side of the hill
from Saul's camp.

CLUES

No one knew or saw David and Abishai because
the Lord had put Saul and
his men into a deep sleep
(1 Samuel 26:12).

He called out to one of Saul's men named Abner, who was in charge of guarding the king. When he answered, David asked Abner why he hadn't protected Saul. He told him that someone had come in the night to destroy Saul. David finished by asking Abner where the king's spear and water jug were.

Saul heard David's voice and called out to him. David asked Saul why he was trying to hunt him down. Saul responded, saying he had sinned and that he wouldn't bring harm to David. Saul also admitted to acting like a fool. David gave Saul back his spear. Saul said that he hoped David would be  blessed and that he knew David would go on to do great things. David went his way, and Saul went back to his home.

Even though David had gotten the better of King Saul and escaped the man's clutches, he still felt like he was going to be captured and harmed. David came up with the plan of escaping into the land of the Philistines, believing that if he did that, then Saul would give up searching for him. David and his band of six hundred men went to a man named Achish, son of the king of Gath. When Saul heard of David's latest move, Saul did not pursue him anymore.

David stayed in the area for more than a year, during which time he went out and captured new towns. Meanwhile, the Philistines began gathering troops to do battle against the Israelites. Achish told David that he would be fighting for the Philistine army. Saul gathered the Israelite army in preparation to fight the Philistines. But he was afraid and "terror filled his heart" (1 Samuel 28:5).

Saul prayed, but the Lord did not answer him.

When the Philistines were about to attack the Israelites, they turned to Achish and told him not to let David fight with them. They were afraid that David would turn on them at the last minute. When they returned home, they found that their city had been raided. David was very sad, but he "found strength in the LORD his God" (1 Samuel 30:6). David prayed and asked God if he should pursue the raiding party, and God said yes.

David went with four hundred men to pursue the Amalekites. Two hundred men stayed behind because they were too exhausted to continue. They came across an Egyptian man who had been abandoned by his master. His master was part of the raiding party that David was trying to catch. The man agreed to show him where the party was. David caught up with them and fought them for a whole day. He recovered everything that had been plundered from his village. And he returned all of it. When the two hundred who stayed behind saw them, they were excited. But some of the four hundred men who went with David and fought did not want to share the plunder. David intervened and said they were going to share because it was the Lord who had provided, and God didn't want His people to be selfish. David sent some of the plunder to people in many towns throughout the area where he and his men had roamed.

Meanwhile, the Philistines continued to attack the Israelites and were in pursuit of Saul. Sadly, they took the life of Jonathan, who had been David's very close friend. It was a fierce battle, but soon the Philistines got to Saul and wounded him very badly. The king asked one of his own men to take his sword and use it on

Saul, but the man did not obey. "Saul took his own sword and fell on it" (1 Samuel 31:4). Once the Israelites received the news that Saul and his family were gone, they fled their towns. And the Philistines took over the land.

David heard about Saul's death when a messenger came and told him the sad news. That's  also when David learned that his dear friend Jonathan had also lost his life. David and his men tore their clothes in frustration and mourned for Saul and Jonathan. Over time, David prayed and asked God what he should do now that Saul was gone.

God told David to go to Hebron, which was a place in the land of Judah. After David and his people moved, the men of Judah came and "anointed David king over the tribe of Judah" (2 Samuel 2:4). One of Saul's other sons, Ish-Bosheth, became king over Israel and reigned for two years. David ruled for seven years as king in Hebron.

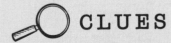 **CLUES**

The kings' armies fought, but David's side won. The Bible says that David continued to grow stronger and stronger, while the house of Saul became weaker and weaker.

6

Becoming King

When David was thirty years old, he became king over Israel. He reigned for forty years. He continued to be successful and even won Jerusalem from his enemies because "the LORD God Almighty was with him" (2 Samuel 5:10).

David defeated the Philistines and then gathered together all the thirty thousand young

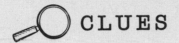

CLUES

The ark of the covenant was a gold-covered wooden chest that had two angels on the cover and contained the two stone tablets of the Ten Commandments. This ark symbolized God's presence, so it was important for David that it was with him and his people in Jerusalem.

men of Israel and brought the ark of the covenant back to Jerusalem.

As time passed, David felt convicted because he didn't think it was right that the ark of God was being housed in a tent while he was living in a palace. There was a prophet named Nathan who was a good friend of David's. When David voiced his concerns, Nathan told David he should do as he pleased because the Lord was with him (2 Samuel 7:3).

David made a habit of praying to God in an act of worship. The Bible records his many victories in battle, and he was blessed in everything he did. Along the way, David had a son named Absalom.

Absalom was not a very nice person, and he set out to take over the power that had been set aside for his father. Absalom would stand by the city gate and intercept the people who had come to talk to David. He promised people justice if they would help get him appointed judge in the land. The Bible says, he "stole the hearts of the people of Israel" (2 Samuel 15:6).

David knew that the people's hearts were turning toward Absalom, so he told his officials that they had to join him in leaving Jerusalem. They went out across the valley and up the Mount of Olives. David and his people continued traveling away from his son, who was trying to take David's life.

Absalom went

 CLUES

This same thing had happened to David with Saul. David was being chased by someone close to him. He was being hunted even though he hadn't done anything wrong.

out in search of David. Meanwhile, David sent troops out to intercept Absalom, but the king told his commanders to "be gentle with the young man Absalom for my sake" (2 Samuel 18:5). A big battle took place between David and Absalom's men in the forest of Ephraim. The fighting spread out across the whole countryside.

As Absalom was riding his mule through the forest, his hair got caught on the branches of a large oak tree. The mule kept going, which caused Absalom to fall off. He was literally hanging by his hair. One of David's men found Absalom and obeyed the king's orders not to bring harm to his son. But another soldier named Joab did not obey, and he quickly found Absalom and took his life. King David eventually got the news of his son's death, and he was very sad (2 Samuel 18:33).

Eventually David returned to his palace in

Jerusalem, but things would not return to normal.
A troublemaker named Sheba didn't want David
to be king, so he started telling the men of Israel
not to have anything to do with the king. For some
reason, they listened and deserted David.

Final Days

For three years famine ravaged the land, and David faced even more battles with enemy lands. But each time God delivered David, and each time David learned more about just how big and mighty God is. In 2 Samuel 22:2–3, David wrote these words:

> "The LORD is my rock, my fortress and

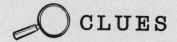

CLUES

Everything David believed had to do with God's wonderful character. At times in his life, David made bad choices, but he always wanted to make his relationship with God better. David made God his refuge, because he knew no other way. David understood that keeping a good connection to God was the best and only way to live a life that honored God.

my deliverer; my God is my rock, in whom I take refuge, my shield and the horn of my salvation. He is my stronghold, my refuge and my savior."

The Bible records the last words of David before he died. This is a small section of those final thoughts:

> "If my house were not right with God, surely he would not have made with me an everlasting covenant, arranged and secured in every part" (2 Samuel 23:5).

David wanted to make sure that things were right between him and God. He wanted to leave a legacy of hope for his people. Even at the end of his life, when he was very old, David had to deal with difficult situations. The Bible says that David's son

Solomon was in line to become king after David. But his other son, Adonijah, appointed himself king instead. David's wife Bathsheba came to tell the king about the problem. Even David's prophet Nathan told the king about the dilemma.

David ordered his priest and prophet to go to Solomon and anoint him the new king. Then they were told to have Solomon come back to the palace to sit on the throne as Israel's new king.

Soon after this, King David's time was near. He took his son Solomon aside and had a very powerful talk. David said, "Be strong, act like a man, and observe what the LORD your God requires: Walk in obedience to him, and keep his decrees and commands" (1 Kings 2:2–3). By the time David finished his work, he had been king over Israel for forty years.

8

Songs

The Psalms in the Bible are actual songs meant to be sung to the Lord in worship. The Bible names David as the author of seventy-three of the one hundred and fifty psalms. While there isn't room to look at all of them in this book, the themes mentioned in these first psalms of David are common and found in all of David's songs.

Psalm 3 is the

CLUES

By looking at some of the psalms David created, we can get a better understanding of who God is and how David talked to Him. The psalms are encouraging and raw in honesty. They help us know that God is always in control and wants to give His children the best He has to offer. God doesn't hold back. He loves us, and His love is overwhelming!

first of the psalms written by David. David was struggling with feeling that God was somewhere else besides in his life. He cried out that his enemies were many and that God wouldn't deliver him from the fray. However, David wouldn't give in to fear and said that God was his shield, the One who lifted his head in times of trouble. David knew God heard his cries for help and that He was the One who sustained him. David wouldn't fear because he knew God loved him.

Psalm 4 is also written by David and shows how the king asked God for mercy and answered prayers. David reminded his audience that God hears us when we call to Him. He also reminded us to trust God and let our hearts be filled with His joy. God covers us with His peace and lets His face shine on us. God alone helps us to live in safety.

In Psalm 5, David asked God to hear his prayer for help. He saw the morning as the time to give all that is on your heart to God and wait on Him to move and answer according to His will. David taught that because of God's great love, we should praise Him. David wanted God to lead him in righteousness and make his way straight. David also sang about taking refuge in God and that God would protect those who love Him and that those people would rejoice. David sang that God surrounds His people like a shield.

In Psalm 6, David asked God for mercy and healing. He cried out that his soul was aching, and he wanted God to deliver him from the pain. The psalms share real emotions, and they were written to communicate a man's heart for his Creator. David called out to God and said he was worn out from groaning. David said he flooded his bed with tears and his eyes were weak from sorrow. The best part was that David knew God heard his prayers.

Psalm 7 shows David taking refuge in God. Again, David cried out to God for help in a stressful situation. David asked for justice and prayed for God to rise up and protect him. And even though David was going through difficult times, he said he would give thanks to God because God is righteous.

Psalm 8 begins with David praising God's holy and majestic name. David stood in awe of the fact that God cared for him. He sang words that remind us that God has given us His amazing grace and glory.

Psalm 9 teaches us to always be thankful for what God has given. David sang that he would tell everyone about how great God is and that he would praise His name. David wrote that his enemies turned away because of God's mighty presence. David said that God held him up. He sang of God's eternal reign. David wanted others to know that God is their refuge and a strong, safe place when trouble comes.

Psalm 11 reminds us that God is righteous and loves justice; and Psalm 12 lets us know that it is okay to call out to God for help. David said that God cares for and protects the poor from evildoers. Many of David's psalms are very emotional and show him crying out to God for reassurance. In Psalm 13, David said to God, "I trust in your unfailing love; my heart rejoices in your salvation. I will sing the Lord's praise, for he has been good to me" (vv. 5–6).

Psalm 14 shows that David wanted people to know God is reliable—He is there for us. David sang that God is our salvation and that God again is our refuge and our everything. And Psalm 15 reminds us what David knew to be important in life. He said that we need to watch how we talk to others and help our friends. We need to honor God with our behavior, even when making the right decision is hard.

9

Now that we've investigated the story of King David, it's time to study some lessons we can learn from his life. We will look at ten Power-Ups that will help us connect scripture to our daily lives. Memory verses go along with each Power-Up to help us plant God's truth in our hearts.

Power-Up #1:

GOD IS STRONG ENOUGH!

When David faced Goliath, he saw the giant as a problem to be solved because the enemy was going against God. David reminds us that our struggles in life belong to God. Jesus has already won the battle! We can't rely on our own strength to handle life's problems. We rely on God, because He is strong enough.

MEMORY VERSE: "It is not by sword or spear that the LORD saves; for the battle is the LORD's." 1 SAMUEL 17:47

Power-Up #2:

GOD LOOKS AT PEOPLE'S HEARTS. WE SHOULD TOO.

When Samuel went to Jesse in search of the next king to anoint for God, Jesse incorrectly assumed one of his older, stronger sons would be the chosen one. But we learn that God doesn't judge by outward appearances.

This is a good principle for us to practice. We have to remember that we can't know anything about a person just by looking at them.

Power-Up #3:

STAND UP FOR GOD.

David became upset when he heard Goliath talking badly about the armies of God. Since David was still very young, King Saul didn't think sending him to fight Goliath was a good idea. That's when David continued to stand up for God by showing Saul he wasn't afraid.

God had rescued David from wild animals after all. So he knew that God was certainly big enough to rescue him from the giant. We can have the same confidence as David as we face our own "giants" in life. We can have the courage to know that God is always with us!

Power-Up #4:
GOD IS WITH YOU.

After David defeated Goliath, the king invited him in to be a part of his team. Saul sent David out on missions, and David was always successful. So Saul gave David a high rank in the army. David found success in *all* the things he did because God was right there with him.

This is a great lesson to remember. God will use you to be a part of His kingdom work. Don't worry about making mistakes. God will go before you to lead the way!

Memory verse: In everything he did he had great success, because the LORD was with him. 1 SAMUEL 18:14

Power-Up #5:
GOD IS IN CONTROL.

David spent many of his days running away from Saul. David could have chosen to handle things differently. But he wanted to honor God, and he knew that God was in control of his life.

We can have this same attitude in our own lives too. We can step out in faith knowing that God is in charge of all our days.

Memory verse: Day after day Saul searched for him, but God did not give David into his hands. 1 SAMUEL 23:14

Power-Up #6:
FIND ALL YOUR
STRENGTH IN GOD.

David made sure he relied on God. For wisdom and strength, David went to his Creator for help. This is like the image of Jesus that's mentioned in the New Testament when Jesus tells the story of how one man built his house on the sand while a second man built his house on the rock.

God is our rock. He is where our strength comes from. Jesus said when the storms of life come, the house built on the rock won't fall down.

Memory verse: David found strength in the LORD his God. 1 SAMUEL 30:6

Power-Up #7:

GOD IS YOUR ROCK!

Like we said in Power-up #6, God is bigger and stronger than we will ever know. When we understand that He is our rock, we know that He is unchanging.

God is our immovable foundation who will never change His mind about us. He loves you, and that's the way it will always be! Rely on God to be there for you all the time.

Memory verse: "The Lord is my rock, my fortress and my deliverer." 2 Samuel 22:2

Power-Up #8:
GOD MAKES YOUR
LIFE SECURE.

God made you, and He loves you very much. He takes every difficult day and makes things better. God is always there to look out for you. He never turns away.

David reminds us to stay connected to God and keep reading the Bible so we will always know what He wants for us. God makes your life secure so you don't have to worry about anything. He's got this!

Memory verse: Spread your protection over them, that those who love your name may rejoice in you. PSALM 5:11

Power-Up #9:

OBEY GOD AND
BE STRONG.

God is calling you to be a big part of His kingdom work. To do a good job, you must understand that God's ways are *always* best.

Obeying God will keep you connected to Him and help you follow the path He has made for you.

Power-Up #10:

GOD GIVES YOU REST.

Just like David wrote his songs from his experiences with God, we can also live each day knowing that God is with us. David was a shepherd, and so he came to see God as his Shepherd. We are God's children, so we can know that God is for us and wants us to have good rest.

Everything we need, God has for us. Everything we look for in life can be found in God. Let this lesson fill your heart with confidence and hope!

Memory verse: The LORD is my shepherd, I lack nothing. He makes me lie down in green pastures, he leads me beside quiet waters, he refreshes my soul. PSALM 23:1-3

Kingdom Files:

Who Was Jonah?

Dear Reading Detective,

Welcome to Kingdom Files! You're now a very important part of the Kingdom Files investigation—a series of really cool biographies all found in the Bible. Each case you investigate focuses on an important Bible character and is separated into three sections to make your time fun and interesting. First, you'll find the **Fact File**, which contains key information about a specific Bible character whom God called to do big things for His kingdom. Next, you'll read through an **Action File** that lays out Bible events showing the character in action. And finally, the **Power File** is where you'll find valuable information and memory verses to help you see how God is working in your life too. Along the way, **Clue Boxes** will offer applications to help you keep track of your thoughts as you make your way through the files. You can also use these sections to record questions you might have along Jonah's journey. Write down any questions, and then ask your parents to get them involved in your quest.

Before you begin, know this: not only did God have plans for the Bible characters you'll read about in the Kingdom Files, but Jeremiah 29:11 says that God has big plans for you too! I pray that *Kingdom Files: Who Was Jonah?* helps you get a bigger picture of God and that you will see just how much He loves you!

Blessings,

M.K.

Name: **JONAH**
Occupation: **prophet**
From: **Gath-Hepher**
(just north of Nazareth)
Years Active: **786–746 BC**

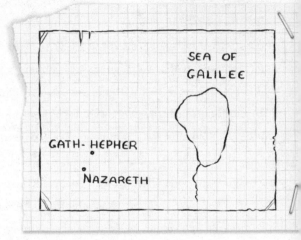

SEA OF
GALILEE

GATH-HEPHER
●

● NAZARETH

Kingdom Work: **preached to the
people of Nineveh**

Mini Timeline:

793 BC
JONAH
BECOMES
A PROPHET

785 BC
JONAH
PREACHES
TO NINEVEH

753 BC
JONAH'S
MINISTRY
ENDS

Key Stats:

+ Called to share
  the gospel with
  his greatest
  enemy

+ Knew God was
  merciful and
  loving

+ Worshipped God
  through prayer

1

Run Away!

God had a very important job for Jonah. He wanted him to be a prophet. A prophet was a person God used to go and tell people important news about His kingdom. This was a very important job because it helped people turn away from selfish living and come back to a strong relationship with God. In many cases, the prophets had to go into uncomfortable situations to let people know they were making bad choices. They had to stand up for God, even when everyone else lost sight of what was truly important.

God talked to Jonah about a very special plan He had for his life. When Jonah heard the plan, he wasn't too happy. Here's why...

There was a really big city called Nineveh (almost five hundred miles away from Israel), and God asked Jonah to go there. The people who lived in Nineveh were not making good choices. In fact, the Bible says that the city was filled with wickedness. Also, Nineveh was the capital city of Assyria, the great and evil empire that was the enemy of Jonah's people. (Would *you* want to go into that city?)

Jonah didn't like God's plan because it meant that he would have to leave his comfort zone and trust God with everything. He didn't want to go to Nineveh, and he really didn't want to tell people what they were doing wrong. So guess what Jonah did? That's right, he ran away! It seems crazy that even though God personally called Jonah to do a big kingdom job, Jonah didn't want any part of it. But after gathering all the facts, we will see that Jonah was human and had many different emotions and concerns. Let's see how God worked in Jonah's life so that we can see the bigger picture of God's love and mercy and how those characteristics change lives.

~~~~~~~~~~

Jonah was the son of a man named Amittai, which means "my truth." Jonah was going to receive a very big job that had everything to do with sharing God's truth.

God wanted Jonah to share His truth in a city called Nineveh. That was one tough place, and Jonah didn't want any part of it. The people there lived life however they wanted and didn't care about God. Nineveh was also a great and powerful city. It was actually the largest city in the world during Jonah's day. That's pretty intimidating.

It didn't matter how wicked the city was, and it didn't mean a whole lot to Jonah that the people there heard the Good News. As far as he was concerned, they didn't deserve to be blessed. Punishment for their bad behavior was what Jonah was hoping for. He didn't want to bother going all that way to some crazy, faraway place just to be ignored.

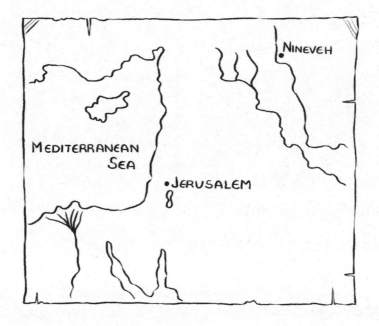

The first thing Jonah did was run away. Not just run across town. Jonah wanted as much distance between himself and Nineveh as possible. Across the sea was a port town called Tarshish. That's exactly where Jonah decided to go. It would get him far away from the bad people so he wouldn't have to deal with the stress of it all.

Jonah had money and used it to buy a ticket for a boat ride that would take him to a distant place that was on the other side of the map

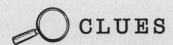

CLUES

Today in our world, there are people who look different and act different than we as believers act. They use bad language and listen to inappropriate songs on the radio and don't care about watching bad shows on TV. They don't believe in God and may even say that Jesus was just a good man but not the world's Savior. As we read Jonah's case, we need to pay attention to how God sees these kinds of people. We need to watch how God wants us to treat them.

from Nineveh. Think about it: God saw Jonah and called him to do a great thing. Jonah knew God was faithful, and he knew how God had taken care of His people in the past. Still, something in Jonah's heart made him panic. He was trusting in what his eyes saw instead of the mighty power of God.

The Bible uses the word *flee* to describe Jonah's actions. He wanted to run the opposite direction from where God was telling him to go. He wanted to hop on a boat and sail across the ocean so he could "flee from the LORD" (1:3).

Jonah hopped aboard a ship that was setting sail for the faraway port called Tarshish. (And this is where Jonah's journey gets interesting.) God sent a great wind over the sea that Jonah's boat was on. The wind blew and grew, twisted and turned, until it became a violent storm.

The storm raged, and the boat was wildly tossed back and forth as the waves crashed, ready to break the boat into pieces. The crew panicked and started throwing their precious cargo overboard, trying to make the ship lighter in hopes that they could save themselves. The cargo was what they would normally sell to make money. But here in the middle of the furious storm, none of that mattered!

As the crew tossed their material possessions overboard, the men were also calling out to their own gods for help. The strange thing is that the wicked storm didn't seem to bother Jonah! The Bible says that while the tempest (that's a razzle-dazzle word for "bad storm") was raging, he made his way below deck and found a nice place to lie down. Can you imagine?

CLUES

This is where Jonah gets his literal and spiritual wake-up call. If you're familiar with Jonah's story, you know a colossal fish was looming deep within the sea below. But this scene with the ship's captain demands your attention to the details.

Remember back at the beginning of our investigation, when we discovered that God was calling Jonah to go to the great city of Nineveh? There was a king in the city (we'll learn more about him later) who would eventually hear Jonah's message about God. If Jonah had obeyed God the first time, he'd have been standing inside the massive city walls, possibly speaking with a king; but instead, Jonah ended up inside the tiny wooden walls of a boat during a storm, while being yelled at by a ship's captain!

Poor Jonah.

A wild hurricane of sorts is spinning around your boat. Grown men are screaming, fearing for their lives. (What would *you* do?)

Well, while all that craziness was going on, Jonah fell asleep. And not just a light take-a-nap sleep. Jonah fell into a "deep sleep" (1:5).

But Jonah couldn't run away any longer. The ship's leader got right to the point. He yelled at Jonah to wake up. He then commanded Jonah to call upon God so that all of them could be saved.

2

Who's Responsible?

Meanwhile, the sailors were back on deck, still trying to figure out who or what was responsible for causing the violent storm. This had to have been the worst storm the sailors had ever seen, because they first tried dumping their precious cargo overboard. That didn't work, so they resorted to a time-honored method for finding answers: casting lots.

"Lots" were either sticks with markings on them or a handful of small, flat stones with symbols on each one. They were tossed into a small area and then interpreted. That's what casting lots meant back in the Bible times.

The men on the boat had to do something, and they had to do it quickly. So the sailors cast lots to see who was responsible for their bad situation. After the stones were tossed onto the deck, "the lot fell on Jonah" (1:7).

The Bible records Jonah trying to avoid the truth even at this point of his story. It was bad enough that he had run away from God the first time. Now, here he was in the middle of the tempest, jeopardizing not only his life but the lives of all the crew, running away from reality. Just like when he had tried to sleep away his problems, Jonah would try and talk his way out of this difficult situation.

The men asked Jonah whose fault gave rise to the storm. They asked him what kind of work he did. They asked him where he came from. "What is your country? Who are your people?" Did Jonah just stand there in silence? It seems so, because he didn't answer at first. He waited until after the men pounded him with their interrogation. And the response Jonah finally gave only answered one of their questions. "I am a Hebrew and I worship the LORD, the God of heaven, who made the sea and the dry land" (1:9).

It sounds like Jonah was telling the men that the storm was God's doing, which we already know is true. As a prophet, it was Jonah's job to stick up for God. Telling the sailors who the real God was helped get things back on track. But doing so came at a price. The sailors were terrified. They immediately asked Jonah what he did wrong to cause all this chaos. The Bible says that Jonah had already told them that he was running away from God. One way or another, the truth comes out. At least Jonah stood up for God sooner rather than later. And at least he stopped running.

But the storm raged on. Just because Jonah told the men about God didn't mean the stressful things in his life were going to suddenly disappear.

As Jonah would learn, things happen according to God's timeline. Jonah had tried to run ahead of God, but instead he would learn about the blessings that come from waiting on God.

The crew got right to the point and asked Jonah what they should do with him. They knew that somehow Jonah and the storm were connected. And since Jonah had made up his mind to stop running from God, he came up with an extreme solution: "Pick me up and throw me into the sea. . . and it will become calm. I know that it is my fault that this great storm has come upon you" (1:12).

Instead of saying he was sorry, Jonah went right for a drastic plan of action.

As it turns out, the sailors responded in an unexpected way. Instead of throwing Jonah over the railing like he was a piece of the cargo, they ignored his request and tried to row the boat back to land. They didn't react in anger. They didn't hurl insults at Jonah and blame him for their nerve-racking situation. The men simply put all their energy into coming up with a peaceful solution to a very difficult problem.

Imagine if you were on that boat. Would you want to be far away from Jonah? The men rowed, but "the sea grew even wilder than before" (1:13). This is where Jonah's disobedience was used for God's glory. Despite how bad the situation looked, inside the hearts of the sailors, wonderful salvation was on its way. They cried out to the one true God! They finally understood how things

should be. They had made a decision to honor Jonah's original request, but they wanted to make sure their hearts were right with God. They didn't want to harm Jonah, but they knew he didn't stand a chance once he landed in the water.

So what happened next?

The sea became calm. Peace covered the water, and the angry waves disappeared. Jonah was drowning, but the sailors were in a place they had never been before. They had just escaped a storm that had been raging in their hearts. The Bible says that they now "greatly feared the Lord, and they offered a sacrifice to the Lord and made vows to him" (1:16).

～～～～～～～

We need to pause and think about all the clues we've gathered in our study so far. God invited

Jonah to preach the Good News to the people of Nineveh. Jonah said "no way" and took off running. The cool thing is that while all that was going on, the sailors were going about their daily routines, getting ready to set sail for another day's journey. They had no idea that a prophet of God was headed in their direction. They had no idea that the worst storm they'd live through was about to rise up.

3

The Monster Fish!

Long before the sailors tossed Jonah into the sea, God was preparing an escape plan for His prophet. Way back in the beginning of time, God was creating the world. In the book of Genesis, we read that God created the "great creatures of the sea" (1:21).

Jesus referred to a huge fish in the gospel of Matthew (12:40). God provided a monster fish to rescue His child. And just like Jesus was in the tomb for three days, so too was Jonah in the belly of the sea creature.

What would you do if you were Jonah? Panic? Sleep? Wonder? Maybe Jonah did all these things, but the Bible doesn't tell us for certain. What it does tell us, though, is that Jonah prayed! We see that Jonah was finally in a place where he could no longer run. He couldn't hide from God. The only thing he had left to do was pour out his heart to his Maker.

What did Jonah say to God? Here in the middle of nowhere—in the middle of the watery depths— Jonah first cried out to God, and God listened. Jonah's story tells us that in the center of his troubles, God provided answers.

There isn't some faraway place where we are beyond God's reach. Jonah said in his prayer that once he hit the water, he went down into the "realm of the dead" (2:2). But a great clue is found here among the words of the prophet's prayer: even though it looked like Jonah's fate was sealed, even though he felt like he was dying, the prophet grabbed on to the hope that

only God can give. Jonah reached out his hands and held on to the One who called his name. The One who is worthy of praise. Again, Jonah said that God listened to him. And what a relief it must have been for Jonah to know, without a doubt, that the God of the universe was there for him!

Real, gritty prayers—those are the kind of prayers Jonah was praying. He admitted that God was the One who threw him into the water,

but he didn't blame God or complain about his situation.

Jonah didn't miss a detail. He mentioned the strong currents swirling around him and said God's waves and breakers crashed over him.

It seems that Jonah had treaded water for quite a while (trying to save himself!) but eventually gave in and allowed himself to be pulled under. And then we get a glimpse of the worst part of Jonah's experience: "I have been banished from your sight" (2:4). Not the sailors. Not the storm. Not even the massive sea monster that swallowed him whole. Scariest for Jonah was actually believing that wherever he was, God had taken His eyes off him.

At Jonah's lowest point, God must have reassured him, because he had an immediate change of heart: "Yet I will look again toward your holy temple" (2:4). What a memorable moment in Jonah's life as he went from the darkness of despair to the glorious light of God's promises!

Praying Hard

Sometimes it takes very difficult circumstances to make prayer something more than a checklist item. Praying not because you just feel like you want to, but crying out to God because you *must*. Jonah was in the belly of the great fish, talking to God about

his terrifying predicament. The prophet had tried to outrun his Creator only to find himself trapped in an ocean of bad decisions and life-changing consequences.

Jonah admitted that for a moment he thought life was over due to the deep ocean water surrounding him. "Seaweed was wrapped around my head" (2:5). Nature was preparing the prophet for a burial at sea. Jonah had sunk down to the darkest depths of the ocean. And there was an enemy lurking in the watery shadows. We know he was there. . .whispering to Jonah that God had surely abandoned him.

Down and down Jonah went until he couldn't sink any deeper. He wrote that he had sunk so far down, he had reached the "roots of the mountains" (2:6). As these events unfolded, it surely seemed that Jonah had run out of options.

But at this point in Jonah's tragedy, God

reached down and saved him. Jonah continued to give God all the credit by reminding us that it was God alone who brought his life up from the pit (2:6). He was telling God all the bad things that He had rescued Jonah from. And Jonah certainly didn't deserve to be rescued. He was the one who had run away from the plans God had for his life. Jonah was the one who had said no to the things God had in store for him. Jonah added that all he had to do, while in the belly of the fish, was think about God and pray.

Jonah also confirmed that God hears our prayers. He said that when his life was fading fast, God heard his cries for help. While his body was sinking, Jonah's prayers were going up to heaven.

CLUES

No matter what you're going through, your heavenly Father sees you and accepts your prayers. That should be as comforting to us today as it was to Jonah.

The prophet also gave a warning to avoid following after things of this world. He reminded us that if we grab on to stuff (worthless idols) in order to make us feel happy, we are turning away from the  love God has for us. Jonah worshipped himself when he made the decision to run away from God. He thought it would be safer to flee, and so he poured all of himself into that plan. He worshipped the idea of being in charge of his life.

But Jonah found something that had been hidden in his heart, and it was a wonderful discovery. He found the desire to praise God. He decided to worship God with "shouts of grateful praise" (2:9). This special statement proclaimed his true heart change. Jonah raised his voice so that his praise would be heard by many. At that moment, he committed to being a promise keeper. He vowed to tell anyone who would listen that "salvation comes from the LORD" (2:9). After Jonah came to this life-changing conclusion, God commanded the fish to spit Jonah out onto the beach. Then and there, the prophet could get back to the job God was calling him to do.

5

On to Nineveh

Jonah had escaped death and was feeling really great. He was a changed man—a man alive and renewed. A man who wasn't interested in running away but instead wanted more than anything to do the things God asked him to do. Jonah wanted to give his life away to do the kingdom work that God had ready for him to do. No more self-worship. No more fear. Jonah was ready to listen to and obey the Lord.

God continued to be faithful. He never left Jonah alone in his disobedience. God forgave him and then provided a second chance for Jonah to be a part of the work He was about to do in Nineveh.

Jonah stood on the shore, free from the burdens of fear and worry. Restored physically and

spiritually to the One who called him to do great things. And so, this is where God called back to Jonah, "Go to the great city of Nineveh" (3:2). Even though this was the second time God told Jonah to go, there was no confusion in Jonah's mind. He was ready to go. He was ready to obey. He was ready to align his heart with God's and

feel the peace that comes from a heart full of hope.

Finally, Jonah made his way to Nineveh. Nothing is recorded in the Bible about the journey he had from where he was on the shore to the great city. But we do know that Jonah desired to get there and start speaking truth to the people of Nineveh.

When Jonah arrived, he was overwhelmed by the sheer size of the city. The Bible said it took a person three whole days to walk through all of Nineveh. Jonah covered as much of the city as he could in one day. Along the way, he told anyone who would listen that their treasured city was going to be overthrown in a little over a month.

God gave the prophet courage and boldness to do the job He called Jonah to do. Jonah gives us a powerful picture of faith as he spoke words that were not easy or pleasant to speak. He didn't speak words that the people wanted to hear, and there must have been people there who heard what Jonah was saying and thought he was completely out of his mind.

Whenever God is involved, things don't always go the way the world thinks they should. In fact, after Jonah walked across one-third of the huge city proclaiming disturbing news, the Bible says that the "Ninevites believed God" (3:5). And they just didn't *say* they believed. They *showed* they believed by declaring a fast. That wasn't all. The people put on coarse, black cloth to show that they were mourning. The Bible says that "all of them, from the greatest to the least, put on sackcloth" (3:5).

Jonah got to see the results of his work.

Everywhere, the people of the great city were saying they were sorry and repenting. Hearts were changing, and Jonah witnessed it all. God was being glorified by the same people who, only hours before, had no idea of the gift they were about to receive.

The King's Response

Imagine you are the great king of Nineveh. Your people are talking. They tell you that a foreign man is walking through your city talking about disaster coming your way soon. Imagine them telling you that everyone in your city is listening to this prophet and even going so far as to put on

dirty sackcloth and seek forgiveness. This behavior is unheard of in your land.

What would you do? See the man as a threat and have him arrested? Tell him he's crazy and have him thrown into prison? Remember, you're in charge, and you don't want the people getting weird ideas. It might cause people to question your authority, and you're the king! You definitely don't want that to happen.

The king of Nineveh did something much different. When he heard the message Jonah was preaching in his city, the king also responded in humility. He too, like his people before him, shed his royal robes and exchanged them for sackcloth. He didn't even wait until Jonah was brought into his palace. And when he was all done humbling himself before God and the world, the king took the final step of humility and sat down in the dirt! The king's actions said that what God had to say was more important than his comfort.

The people of Nineveh had already humbled themselves after hearing Jonah's message. And even though the Bible doesn't give details, the

messenger who delivered the news to the king might have added a word or two about the people's reactions. The king probably heard that his whole city was on its knees, repenting before the God of the Israelites.

Either way, the important thing is that the king's transformation was all about his heart. The king wasn't just doing what his people did. The Bible says that he had been sitting on his throne when the

news about Jonah came to him. And the hard, dirty ground became

the king's new command post.

From that lowly position, the king issued a new decree. He said that he didn't want any person or animal to eat or drink. Then he added the command that all people and animals should be covered in sackcloth! Even the animals! (Can you believe that?)

And the king didn't stop there. He commanded everyone in the city to "call urgently on God" (3:8). He said that everyone needed to stop acting ugly and hurting each other. The leader was telling the people that they needed to do business with the only true God. The king had spoken. His response was an act of love for his people because God had stirred his heart to seek forgiveness and restoration.

The king's heart was turned toward God's. He was beginning to understand the attributes of the Father. He said in his decree that he knew God had a compassionate heart and that his hope was in Him.

A new rain of salvation washed over the land. True freedom was on its way to the people of Nineveh. After everything they did to make themselves humble, the Bible says that God saw their actions. It says that God watched as the people "turned from their evil ways" (3:10). Most of all, God held back and didn't bring the destruction that was set to fall over them.

The whole city had heard the Good News. It was time to celebrate, but Jonah was anything but happy!

7

Jonah's Anger

An unbelievable thing had happened. The biggest and meanest city in the land humbled itself and received God's forgiveness! The great city of Nineveh had turned from its bad choices and decided to follow God. But as they were celebrating, the prophet Jonah was quite upset!

It doesn't make sense, does it? Jonah had just had an amazing transformation inside the fish. He had prayed an amazing prayer about how God had saved him and how good life is when you turn to God's love.

But for some reason, it wasn't enough to keep Jonah's emotions together. Maybe he was exhausted from all the traveling and preaching. Whatever it was, Jonah became angry. He felt it was wrong that all the people of Nineveh had sought forgiveness.

Even though his behavior is opposite of what someone might expect, Jonah prayed. He didn't run away again. He talked to God about how he was feeling. He told God that it was the reason he ran away. Jonah said that he wanted to run away to "forestall," or prevent, this outcome (4:2). Jonah knew God's will was best. He knew that his actions weren't going to change the hearts of a nation. That it was all up to God.

Jonah was just being honest and open. He couldn't believe the city that once did its own thing was now praising and praying to Jonah's God. It just didn't feel right to the prophet. So, in his confusion and emotional distress, Jonah decided to list some of God's many attributes. It was all he could do to make things work out with waves of

conflicting feelings crashing over his soul.

Jonah started off by saying that God was gracious. Jonah knew that above all, his heavenly Father was the ultimate grace giver. Jonah had just experienced that grace in back-to-back scenarios: first with the fish and then in the miraculous conversion of Nineveh. Even though Jonah was mentally exhausted, he wanted to speak the truth: God is full of grace.

Jonah also said that compassion is another one of God's important attributes. God cares about His people. God's heart is for His children.

Next, Jonah said that God is slow to anger. Jonah was understanding that God is patient with us. God called Jonah to minister for His kingdom and glory, but Jonah ran away. God didn't get angry with Jonah. He pursued him, meaning God kept following Jonah and never left his side. God kept inviting Jonah to join Him and was there to rescue Jonah when he needed help.

And God is always abounding in love. Jonah knew that he served a God who doesn't love like humans do: God's heart overflows with love in an unending waterfall of mercy and desire.

Finally, God relented from sending calamity. God waited and held back. He is the God who seeks relationships, and Jonah also witnessed this in his brief time in Nineveh.

In another turn of emotions, Jonah asked the Lord to take him away. Jonah would rather have been with God in heaven than have to deal with all the emotions that came with the job of preaching in the big city.

God replied with a question: "Is it right for you to be angry?" (4:4). He wasn't going to turn His back on Jonah. He wouldn't leave Jonah alone because the prophet had an emotional breakdown. That's what the enemy wanted: division and separation.

The Bible doesn't include Jonah's response. All we know is that Jonah left the city and found a place to sit down somewhere to the east. He made a shelter for himself and rested in its shade. Jonah stayed there and "waited to see what would happen" to Nineveh (4:5).

8

God's Gift

Jonah's story has two parts: all the things Jonah decided to do for himself and then the things he did for God.

The wonderful ending is what God did for the

weary prophet. God didn't end the story by judging Jonah or getting mad at him. No, that is not how God operates. God doesn't condemn; He provides. "Then the LORD God provided a leafy plant and made it grow up over Jonah" (4:6). God saw the shelter Jonah had fashioned for himself and wanted to give His child more. And God not only gave Jonah better comfort in the moment but also continued to provide comfort for him.

God also wanted to ease Jonah's pain. He didn't want Jonah to worry or fear. He didn't want Jonah to go to some faraway land and suffer. God gave to Jonah, despite his disobedience and temper tantrums.

If Jonah's story were a Hollywood movie, it would end here. There would be no more

CLUES

Remember that God is gracious. He acts and blesses not because of what people do but because of who He is.

investigation into Jonah's life. Jonah would live happily ever after. But God had a lesson for Jonah to learn. God wanted Jonah to become more and more like Him as he traveled life's journey (which is what God wants for all His children). So God "provided a worm, which chewed the plant so that

it withered" (4:7).

Jonah's shade was taken away, but God didn't stop there. God "provided a scorching east wind" (4:8). The elements became harsh, and Jonah began to feel faint. For the second time, Jonah responded to God by saying he was ready to die.

God challenged Jonah again and asked if he should really be upset about the plant dying. And Jonah very directly said that he had every right to be angry and that he wished his life were over.

God responded in such a wonderful way. Jonah was about to hear that he had been looking at life through the wrong lens. God wanted His prophet to listen to what was really important in life. God was about to tell Jonah that the most important lesson he needed to learn was that people matter. And not only that people matter but that their hearts are not something to ignore or walk away from after a brief interaction. God wanted Jonah to see the permanence of living a life in relationship with all His children.

First, God reminded Jonah that he had done nothing with the plant. Jonah hadn't created it or taken care of it. The prophet had invested nothing, so he should not have been concerned with it.

Second, God was trying to show Jonah that people are more important than things. God wanted Jonah to focus on the fact that the people of Nineveh were so much more important than a plant.

Finally, God taught Jonah that He cares about all people, even those who are spiritually lost and, like children, "cannot tell their right hand from their left" (4:11).

This is where the story of Jonah comes to an

end. Now it's time in our investigation to see what lessons we can take away from Jonah's adventures.

9

Jonah had a gritty, emotional, easy-to-understand story. As we finish our investigation of God's honest prophet, there are several lessons that God would have us take away from our time learning about Jonah's life. We are all called to spread God's truth. Jesus is the Way, the Truth, and the Life. If He is your Savior, then you are His child, and you too are also a son or daughter of Truth! As we looked at the Kingdom File on Jonah, we uncovered many clues that show just how much God cares for His children. And not only that, but we saw over and over again that God cares for all people. God wanted the people in Nineveh, who were really messing up their lives, to hear about His love and saving power. The story of Jonah also shows us that God never walks away from His children. He doesn't talk to us one minute and then take off the next. He is a loving Father who has great plans for us. Now, just like Jonah, sometimes we have a hard time believing what God says; but in the end, we are called to live a life of faith and believe that God's plans are the best. For example, God could have prevented Jonah from getting on the boat, but we saw that God used Jonah's life to reach even more than just the people of Nineveh. God waited for Jonah to get on the boat because the sailors on the boat needed to see truth too.

How comforting to know that God is always there for us. He hears us when we call on Him, and He provides ways out even on the darkest days.

Power-Up #1:
OBEY GOD.

God wants the best for His children. And part of our exploration of Jonah's story shows us that everything God says comes to pass. In one way or another, God's will is always done, and it's always for His glory. We have the opportunity and blessing to see Jonah's story from the vantage point of the finish line, looking back over the course of his journey. We can sit here and say, "If only Jonah had obeyed God the first time instead of running away to Tarshish!"

So, today, take note of this important lesson to help you avoid having regrets. Don't get caught on the wrong end of the "What if?" question.

Power-Up #2:

DON'T BE AFRAID.

When Jonah first heard of God's plan, he thought it was crazy. The prophet knew that Nineveh was filled with wickedness, and he didn't want any part of that city. On some level, the prophet was probably afraid. He must have temporarily forgotten that God was so much bigger than the great city that was the cause of Jonah's anxiety. We need to continue living each of our days praying and reading God's Word. And when we hear God speak a certain plan for our lives, we need to be fearlessly obedient!

MEMORY VERSE: "Be strong and courageous. Do not be afraid; do not be discouraged, for the LORD your God will be with you wherever you go." JOSHUA 1:9

Power-Up #3:
GOD CARES.

God cares about His children. He valued Jonah and saw worth in him. God wanted to use him to do big things for His kingdom. Yes, God knew Jonah was going to run away toward Tarshish, but the beautiful part of the story is that God didn't let Jonah go. God cared for His prophet by sending storms. The change in weather that, at first glance, seemed like a sinister punishment was really a gentle nudge to bring the prophet back on track.

God wanted to have a caring relationship with Jonah. And the way God was always there for Jonah is the exact same way God is here for us today!

MEMORY VERSE: You have searched me, LORD, and you know me. You know when I sit and when I rise; you perceive my thoughts from afar. You discern my going out and my lying down; you are familiar with all my ways. Before a word is on my tongue you, LORD, know it completely. You hem me in behind and before, and you lay your hand upon me. PSALM 139:1-5

Power-Up #4:
GOD LOVES.

The Maker of the universe doesn't need help, but He does choose to have His people be a part of His kingdom work. It didn't matter how Jonah reacted to his situations—God didn't change His plans because Jonah threw a fit. Instead, God continued to love Jonah despite the prophet's ever-changing moods. And God met Jonah with love on every step of his journey. From graciously listening to his prayers to providing for all his needs, God loved Jonah—and today He showers us with the same kind of love. It's a love that calls, fulfills, and best of all remains. This should inspire us to know that we too are filled with God's love as we live life with Him!

MEMORY VERSE: Whoever does not love does not know God, because God is love.
1 JOHN 4:8

Power-Up #5:

GOD IS FAITHFUL.

Because we know that God is faithful, we also need to understand that He never leaves us alone. We have an enemy named Satan who tries to make us believe lies. God proves Himself faithful all the time. There isn't a moment when God loses control or steps off His throne. The Bible says that the enemy is a good deceiver and wants us to feel forgotten and unloved. But the Bible also says that Jesus died for every one of our mistakes because God loves us so much. This makes us feel better on those days when nothing seems to be going right.

MEMORY VERSE: God is faithful, who has called you into fellowship with his Son, Jesus Christ our Lord. 1 CORINTHIANS 1:9

Power-Up #6:

LIVE BY FAITH.

Because God is faithful, we need to live each day and each hour by faith—no matter how hard life may get. The fact that Jonah finally went to Nineveh despite originally wanting to run far away shows that he understood that living life while remaining anchored to God's will is the very best way to live. Imagine Jonah standing on the beach after the fish spit him out on the sand, taking a deep breath as he looked toward Nineveh. Maybe he said something like, "Okay, God. Thank You for saving me. I'm sorry I tried running away. I still don't feel like going to Nineveh, but now I'm ready to do things Your way." Maybe Jonah exhaled and took his first step toward the big, intimidating city. But still Jonah put all his faith in his God, who went before him.

MEMORY VERSE: I have been crucified with Christ and I no longer live, but Christ lives in me. The life I now live in the body, I live by faith in the Son of God, who loved me and gave himself for me. GALATIANS 2:20

Power-Up#7:

PRAY HARD.

Another big lesson we can learn from Jonah's story is that talking to God through prayer shouldn't always be simply asking God for things. God deserves more from us. Praying hard means that we also use our conversations with God to glorify His holy name as we tell Him what He's done for us. For example, instead of something like, *God, please help me not to feel scared*, we can change things up and pray, *God, You are*

Almighty. All throughout the Bible, You have protected people and given them the courage to be brave. Please help me not to feel scared. Remember, the enemy doesn't want us to pray. He would rather we disconnect from God and do our own thing. Commit to praying hard and staying connected to the One who loves His people more than anything.

MEMORY VERSE: This is the confidence we have in approaching God: that if we ask anything according to his will, he hears us. 1 JOHN 5:14

Power-Up #8:
GOD IS GRACE.

Oh, how blessed we are that God gives us grace instead of what we truly deserve. Jonah's story is overflowing with examples of God's grace given at all the right times. When Jonah took off running, God showed him grace by going after Jonah. When Jonah said no, God still showed him grace. When the storm came and threatened to sink the sailors' boat, Jonah used the opportunity to be honest with God.

As Jonah was being tossed in the sea, God was there to catch him in a wave of grace. The enemy is doing everything in his power to make us feel like we're one mistake away from God shaking His head and walking away from us. But this isn't truth. God is grace. Forever. And when we mess up, God is there to show us grace. Live your life full of thankfulness for everything God has done and is doing, because He is grace.

MEMORY VERSE: Let us then approach God's throne of grace with confidence, so that we may receive mercy and find grace to help us in our time of need. HEBREWS 4:16

Power-Up #9:

GOD DOESN'T ABANDON.

What a comforting thought to know that God will never leave us alone. No matter what we are going through, God wants us to understand that He won't walk away from us. He doesn't change. Remember, the enemy wants us to believe that God doesn't care about us. Satan wants us to think that our unanswered prayers are proof that God has gone away and left us to figure things out on our own. But Jonah's story shows that what looked like God's abandonment—the storm, the giant fish, even Nineveh—was actually a blessing sent from God to provide a way for Jonah to become closer to his heavenly Father.

MEMORY VERSE: God has said, "Never will I leave you; never will I forsake you." HEBREWS 13:5

Power-Up #10:
GOD PROVIDES.

As we've seen many times in our investigation of Jonah's story, God is with His prophet at every turn, providing just what Jonah needs, just when he needs it. The Bible says many times that we shouldn't worry; and Jesus even tells us that we shouldn't worry, because He provides. First the storm, then the great fish, then the plant for shade—God gave Jonah just what he needed, right when he needed it. These three gifts were forms of protection, but God also provided purpose for Jonah. He called him to share the Good News with Nineveh, providing Jonah with a job that mattered in God's kingdom. God also provided opportunities for Jonah. The whole Nineveh experience gave Jonah a chance to be an important part of God's mission. Remember that God also gives us what we need when we need it. It may not seem like God is answering our prayers, but He will always provide for us in His time.

MEMORY VERSE: "But seek his kingdom, and these things will be given to you as well." LUKE 12:31

Kingdom Files:
Who Was Daniel?

Dear Reading Detective,

Welcome to Kingdom Files! You're now a very important part of the Kingdom Files investigation—a series of really cool biographies all found in the Bible. Each case you investigate focuses on an important Bible character and is separated into three sections to make your time fun and interesting. First, you'll find the **Fact File**, which contains key information about a specific Bible character whom God called to do big things for His kingdom. Next, you'll read through an **Action File** that lays out Bible events showing the character in action. And finally, the **Power File** is where you'll find valuable information and memory verses to help you see how God is working in your life too. Along the way, **Clue Boxes** will offer applications to help you keep track of your thoughts as you make your way through the files. You can also use these sections to record questions you might have along Daniel's journey. Write down any questions, and then ask your parents to get them involved in your quest.

Before you begin, know this: not only did God have plans for the Bible characters you'll read about in the Kingdom Files, but Jeremiah 29:11 says that God has big plans for you too! I pray that *Kingdom Files: Who Was Daniel?* helps you get a bigger picture of God and that you will see just how much He loves you!

Blessings,

M.K.

Name: **DANIEL**

Occupation: **prophet**

From: **Jerusalem**

Years Active: **605–536 BC**

Kingdom Work: **served as a prophet to the people of Judah, who were being held captive in Babylon**

Mini Timeline:

605 BC
Taken
captive to
Babylon

586 BC
Jerusalem
destroyed

553 BC
Daniel's
first
vision

536 BC
Daniel's
ministry
ends

Key Stats:

+ Stayed commit-
  ted to God even
  though times
  were tough

+ Did his kingdom
  work for seventy
  years in a foreign
  land

+ Trusted God with
  everything

1

In Training

Times were tough. Life as everyone knew it in Jerusalem was flipped upside down after a foreign king came to town and commanded his troops to take over the land.

Besiege, actually. That's a fancy word that means to surround a city with soldiers in order to capture it.

Can you imagine? You and your family are taken captive and forced to move

CLUES

Daniel was part of the royal family in Jerusalem and therefore from the line of King David. (Jesus would come from this same line too.) And even though Daniel had his world wrecked, he never used it as an excuse to walk away from God. In fact, he used it to get closer to Him.

far away and obey a new set of rules. Everything you own is taken from you. You have to start life all over again, afraid and uncertain of the future. That's exactly what happened to Daniel.

Daniel was a very smart young man. And even with all his knowledge, Daniel still rested in God's will and not his own. In addition to these admirable qualities, Daniel was also a pro at understanding people's dreams with God's help, and he led an extremely righteous life—always ready to obey the laws of the Lord.

~~~~~~~~~~

The name Daniel means "God has judged." This is very interesting because even though the Babylonians took Daniel and the Israelites captive,

Daniel means:

GOD HAS JUDGED

God had already mapped out their victory. God had big plans for Daniel. Daniel was in captivity for seventy years, and the great prophet used every one of those years to do bold kingdom work for God's glory.

Our investigation into the life of Daniel begins with an epic invasion. Daniel lived in Jerusalem when the Babylonian king Nebuchadnezzar invaded.

Daniel plus countless other Jewish people were forced from their homes and made to travel nearly a thousand miles to the city of Babylon. All of the world's nations bowed down to Nebuchadnezzar. That's a pretty powerful position to hold! But this earthly kingdom, despite its power and influence, would be no match for God's glorious kingdom. In captivity, Daniel served under the rule of four different kings. Kings rule for only a short time and then they are gone, but God's kingdom lasts forever!

Daniel was carried away from everything he knew and taken to a strange land with a foreign language and many different customs. This new culture was overwhelming, but Daniel made the most of a truly bad situation.

Once Daniel arrived in Babylon, the king ordered him to be brought into his service. Now, Daniel wasn't called by name, but he did fit the description that Nebuchadnezzar was looking for: young, physically fit, handsome, smart, and good at learning new things. There were three other young men who were named in Daniel's story— Hananiah, Mishael, and Azariah. If you're familiar with this story, you might remember that they were given new names—Shadrach, Meshach, and Abednego (see Daniel 1:7).

For the first three years in Babylon, Daniel and his three new friends were given a new education. They were expected to learn the language and

literature of the new culture. And after three years of training, the young men would then be ready to be in the service of the king. In addition to the good education they would receive, the king also decided to share his food, giving Daniel and the students daily meals and wine from his table.

But Daniel, being a child of God, realized that this went against his desire to respect God and His laws. So Daniel asked an official if they could have something else to eat.

This stressed out the official because he was

afraid that if Daniel and the other young men didn't eat the good food from the king, they would become unhealthy. Daniel acted in faith and requested that the official let them do a test. Daniel and his friends would eat only vegetables and drink only water for ten days and then be compared to the others who were eating from the king's table. The Bible says that God caused the official to show Daniel favor and thus allowed the challenge.

Remember that God had big plans for Daniel.

God was with Daniel, and so when the ten days were over, Daniel and company looked "healthier and better nourished than any of the young men who ate the royal food" (1:15). After that, Daniel and the others were allowed to eat their vegetables and drink water so they would not go against God's instructions for their lives.

The young men continued on in their studies, but it was God who gave them "knowledge and understanding of all kinds of literature and learning" (1:17). God gave them an abundance of what they  needed to do His kingdom work. When God blesses, He does it abundantly. And when Daniel and his three friends were presented to the king,

Nebuchadnezzar could find no one else who was equal to them. The Bible says they were "ten times better than all the magicians and enchanters in his whole kingdom" (1:20). That's some pretty powerful God-sized training!

A Very Interesting Dream

While Daniel's training was going on, the king was beginning to have some problems of his own. The Bible says "his mind was troubled and he could not sleep" (2:1). The King had many dreams, and they were so unbelievable that he couldn't figure out what they meant. Nebuchadnezzar called in some people to help him figure things out. He summoned magicians and enchanters as well as sorcerers and astrologers who were put together on his "dream team."

Imagine this group standing before the king. They were looking at each other and wondering what job they were about to be given by the highest authority in the land. The king told them that he'd had dreams, but one in particular was especially bothering him because he had no clue what it meant. The group of astrologers stepped forward and said that if the king would tell them the dream, then they would surely be able to interpret it for him.

But instead of describing his dream, the king told the astrologers that they must figure out what his dream was as well as what it meant. And if they couldn't, they would lose their lives and all their houses would be "turned into piles of rubble" (2:5). The king was surely stressed out at this point. He then told the men that if they were able to tell him the dream and interpret it correctly, they would receive gifts and high honors.

The reply? Again, the group said that all they needed was for the king to tell them the details of the dream, and then they would be glad to explain its meaning. But the king wasn't convinced. He thought they were stalling. He reminded them that there was going to be a penalty if they couldn't come up with an answer. They said, "There is no one on earth who can do what the king asks!" (2:10). The men said that only the "gods" could tell the king what he wanted to know (2:11).

Nebuchadnezzar became so furious that he ordered all the wise men in the entire land to be put to death. And that included Daniel and his friends!

When the king's guard met with Daniel, he was in for quite a surprise. Daniel boldly asked why the king would make such an irrational decision just because the wise

 **CLUES**

Daniel and his friends were taken against their will and made to travel a very great distance where they had to start life all over again in a new culture. But God never left Daniel's side. Remember that God allowed the official to grant Daniel's request for the special diet. With the king's dream, God was setting things up so He could use Daniel in a mighty way for His kingdom plans.

men couldn't tell what his dream entailed. After the man explained the situation, Daniel went directly to the king himself. Talk about courage! Daniel asked for time to be able to interpret the

king's dream, and by God's mercy, the king agreed.

Daniel urged his friends to join him in pleading for mercy from God and to ask God for help. Daniel prayed first. Even though his life and the lives of his three friends were on the line, Daniel didn't panic. He prayed and talked to God. He asked God for help, and he was about to get it in a huge way.

That night while Daniel was asleep, God gave him a vision that outlined the king's dream and the meaning of it as well. When Daniel woke up, he didn't waste a single minute. He prayed again and lifted up praise to thank God for what He did.

Daniel's praise listed some of God's attributes that can help us better understand who God really is. Daniel started off by saying that the name of God should be praised forever. His name is worthy of glory and honor. God is wise and powerful. God changes the times and seasons. He raises up kings and takes them off thrones. He is a wisdom giver.

"Light dwells with him" (2:22). Then Daniel said that God gave him wisdom and power.

Armed with knowledge and answers, Daniel raced to the king's official and told him to stop getting rid of the wise men. God literally used Daniel to

CLUES

Think about it: God gives who He is. So when we feel unloved, God gives us His real love because that's who He is! If we feel discouraged, God gives courage because that's who He is!

save lives, physically and spiritually. The official took Daniel to the king. It was showtime!

The king asked Daniel the same thing he had asked his wise men; and Daniel had a similar, yet completely different, reply. He, like the men earlier, said that no one could do what the king was asking. But unlike the wise men, Daniel said there is a "God in heaven who reveals mysteries" (2:28).

First, Daniel told the king that his dream was about things to come. Daniel made it clear that he didn't get this information because he was better than anybody else, but rather because God would allow Nebuchadnezzar to understand the dream. Remember that this is the same king who had captured Daniel and his friends and so many more people. This is the same king who had seized Jerusalem. Why would Daniel or God want to help him?

The king had dreamed of a huge statue. The head of the statue was made of gold, its chest and arms were silver, its stomach and thighs were made of bronze, its legs were iron, and the feet were a mixture of iron and baked clay. (It was a really weird dream!)

Daniel then told the king that he saw a rock come and smash the statue's feet, which caused the whole statue to crumble into a million pieces.

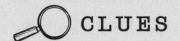

CLUES

Can you imagine the king's reaction? Here's Daniel, one of the people he captured, telling him not only his dream but that God was the One who allowed Daniel to know it! And now for the big explanation of the dream. The king was really in for a big shocker when Daniel started telling him what it all meant.

The wind came and blew all the pieces away so that no one would ever know the statue even existed. And in the final part of the king's dream, the rock grew up to become "a huge mountain" that "filled the whole earth" (2:35).

Then Daniel began to explain the meaning of the king's dream. Daniel respectfully said that Nebuchadnezzar was the king of kings. In other words, he was the biggest guy on the block. Again, Daniel added that the king was where he was because God had given all of it to him. Everyone in the world at that time came under the ruling power of the king. King Nebuchadnezzar was the head of gold. This all sounded good to the king—at least for a moment.

Daniel went on to explain that the rest of the statue represented other kingdoms that would rise up and take Babylon's place. And during their reigns, God would set up a kingdom "that will never be destroyed, nor will it be left to another people. It will crush all those kingdoms and bring them to an end, but it will itself endure forever" (2:44).

Whoa! That's some heavy interpreting that Daniel pulled off all because God was there to help him.

So what do you think the king would do with this new information? The Bible says he fell prostrate on the ground before Daniel to honor him. He also put Daniel in a high place and let him rule over all Babylon. He gave Daniel a ton of gifts, put him in charge of all the wise men, and appointed his friends Shadrach, Meshach, and Abednego to become administrators to help Daniel.

Things began to look up for the prophet.

3

The Golden Statue

With God's help, Daniel stepped
up and delivered exactly what
the king needed to hear. After
learning what his strange dream
meant, it seemed likely that
Nebuchadnezzar would wake
up and realize that his kingdom
wasn't going to last forever. But
instead, he took his dream and
used it as a blueprint to create
a massive golden statue—
ninety feet tall by nine feet
wide, to be exact. And unlike the
dream, the king called for the
whole statue to be made of gold.

He had it built out on the "plain of Dura in the province of Babylon" (3:1). For some reason, the king didn't care about God, even though he had just experienced the dream interpretation with Daniel. And King Nebuchadnezzar summoned all his leaders from across the empire to the unveiling ceremony.

After all the people had gathered in front of the idol, a herald gave the order that when the musicians started playing their instruments, everyone was to "fall down and worship the image" (3:5). If anybody refused, they would be thrown into a fiery furnace so big that grown men could walk in it. Archaeologists believe the main use of this furnace was to make bricks.

When the music started, everyone on the plain fell down and worshipped the golden statue. But remember Daniel's three friends,

Shadrach, Meshach, and Abednego? Well, apparently someone caught them not bowing down and worshipping the idol, and this news was immediately reported to the king. These men loved God and had made a commitment not to be disrespectful and not to worship anything but Him.

When he heard the news, the king became "furious with rage" (3:13) and called for the three men to be brought before him. Nebuchadnezzar asked them if the report was true, and they said it was. The king didn't wait for them to explain. He just continued on and repeated the command that they were to bow down to the statue when the music started, and he said that it would be good for them to obey. Then the king asked what god would save them from the fire if they didn't bow down.

They said, "We do not need to defend ourselves

before you in this matter. If we are thrown into the blazing furnace, the God we serve is able to deliver us from it" (3:16–17). They even said that if God chose not to save them from the flames, still they would never worship the king's golden idol.

The king grew even more furious than before. *How dare these three men disobey me?* he thought. So Nebuchadnezzar ordered the oven to be heated up seven times hotter than normal. And if that wasn't enough, he also ordered some of his strongest soldiers to tie the men up. The king didn't want to leave any room for error.

But as the soldiers took the men to the furnace, the flames killed the soldiers but not Daniel's three friends. The Bible says that even though they fell into the fire, they were not burned!

And when the king looked into the furnace, he couldn't believe his eyes! Not only were the three men still alive, despite the raging flames, but there was a fourth man in the oven with them! The fourth man was "unbound and

unharmed" and looked like "a son of the gods" (3:25). It's not clear whether it was an angel or Jesus in the furnace with them, but God had made a way for the men to be saved.

The king called for the men to come out of the furnace. All the officials who had bowed down to the statue were now gathered around and staring in amazement. "The fire had not harmed their bodies, nor was a hair of their heads singed; their robes were not scorched, and there was no smell of fire on them" (3:27).

God had saved His servants! The king was spellbound. He proclaimed that God should be honored among all the nations. Nebuchadnezzar wasn't done with his idol worship, though. He was just telling the world that Daniel's God was powerful and that no one should speak against Him. Either way, the king promoted Daniel's three friends to high positions within the province of Babylon.

More Dreams and New Kings

The king was really getting some good nights of sleep, because right after the fiery furnace drama, he was back to having strange dreams. His next

dream was about an enormous tree. Nebuchadnezzar watched as the tree grew very tall and very strong. It grew and grew until it touched the sky and could be seen from all the ends of the earth. "Its leaves were beautiful, its fruit abundant, and on it was food for all" (4:12). Wild animals found shelter under the tree, and many birds made homes in its branches. The tree provided food for all the creatures.

In the next part of the dream, the king saw a messenger come down from heaven and issue an order for the tree to be cut down and trimmed of its branches, be stripped of all its leaves, and have the fruit thrown out in every direction. The tree could no longer be a home for all the wild

animals. The only things that were to remain were the stump and roots. Also, the dreamer was to live with the animals.

The king called for Daniel to do his job and offer a meaning for this new dream. But Daniel was nervous because he soon realized that the dream wasn't about the king's enemies. The dream was about the king himself! Daniel explained all the positives first—the king was great, and his rules extended all the way to the ends of the earth. But then Daniel told the king that he would be taken away from his subjects and would be made to eat the grass of the fields just like an ox. The king would stay this way until he acknowledged that God was the true sovereign king.

It took awhile for the dream to be fulfilled, but a year later the king was walking on the roof of his palace, making comments about how all he could see came by the work of his hands. As soon as he spoke these words, the Bible says Nebuchadnezzar heard a voice call down from heaven and tell him that his authority was being pulled from him, and he was about to be sent out to live with wild animals for seven years! His hair and nails grew so

long, the king started to look like a wild animal himself. He even began to lose his mind.

But at the end of the seven years, the king lifted his eyes to heaven, and then his sanity was restored. King Nebuchadnezzar began to praise God and give Him glory. He said that God's "dominion is an eternal dominion" and "his kingdom endures from generation to generation" (4:34). Then he got his throne back and admitted that he was an even greater king than before. Nebuchadnezzar said that God humbles the prideful.

Later, the king stepped down and his son, Belshazzar, became the new king. He had a big dinner party with a thousand guests. During the festivities, the new king ordered the gold and silver goblets that his father had taken from the temple in Jerusalem be brought in so they could drink from them. As they were drinking from them, the Bible says they began praising the gods of gold, silver, bronze, iron, wood, and stone.

As this was going on, the fingers of a hand appeared and began writing on one of the palace walls! The king became afraid. "His legs became weak and his knees were knocking" (5:6). Then, just like his father before him, Belshazzar called in all his people to see if they could tell him what it meant. He offered them a purple robe and a gold chain and even a very high position of authority. But no one could explain what the writing on the wall meant.

At this point, the queen came in and said not to worry because there was a man named Daniel in the kingdom who could help. She relayed everything that Daniel did to help Nebuchadnezzar and claimed that Daniel could help the new king too.

So Daniel was brought in before the king and offered the gifts for a correct interpretation. Daniel told the king to keep the gifts and give them to someone else but that he would help explain the writing.

The first thing Daniel did was remind Belshazzar all about his father's experiences on the throne. He talked about how his heart became prideful and he was forced to live like a wild animal until he came to the place where he acknowledged God as the sovereign ruler of all the earth. Then Daniel said that Belshazzar knew all this and still didn't humble himself. He said that God holds the king's life in his hands and that he was acting very disrespectful to God by praising the other gods.

And then Daniel spoke about the writing: MENE, MENE, TEKEL, UPHARSIN.

He said, "*Mene:* [means] God has numbered the days of your reign and brought it to an end. *Tekel:* [means] You have been weighed on the scales and found wanting" (5:26–27). "Found wanting" means that people weren't living like they should and needed to change their behavior. Daniel went on, "*Peres:* [means] Your kingdom is divided and given to the Medes and Persians" (v. 28).

The king was satisfied with Daniel's interpretation and gave him a purple royal robe, a really nice gold chain, and a very important job. Daniel was promoted to third highest ruler in the kingdom! He didn't do all the interpreting for the gifts, but since Daniel loved to stay connected with God, his words to the new king came from his desire to see more people know God.

That very night the king's life was taken by the enemy, and a man named Darius the Mede took over the kingdom.

Lions!

One of the first things the new king did was appoint new mini-rulers throughout the land, called satraps, to make sure his kingdom would be protected. Then Darius appointed three administrators to look over the satraps—one of them was Daniel. In fact, Daniel was so respected that the new king wanted to put him in charge of the whole kingdom.

The other administrators and rulers didn't like this at all and immediately tried to find ways to get Daniel kicked out. But they had a big problem because Daniel was "trustworthy and neither corrupt nor negligent" (6:4).

The men had to get creative. So they decided to go to the king and recommend that he come up with a new law. The new law would make it a crime to pray to anyone except the king for a month! And the punishment for the "crime"? Getting thrown into the lions' den! The king listened to the men and put the new law in writing.

When Daniel heard of this new law, he went home and prayed like he always did, giving thanks to God. Then men followed Daniel and caught him praying to God for help. They quickly went back to the king and told him that Daniel had disobeyed the law. The king cared for Daniel, and he tried to save him from the punishment of the lions' den.

The men reminded the king that a law is a law, so King Darius ordered Daniel be sent to the lions' den. The king said to Daniel, "May your God, whom you serve continually, rescue you!" (6:16). Then the king had a stone rolled in front of the den opening so Daniel couldn't escape. He returned to the palace worried about Daniel. He couldn't eat or sleep.

As soon as the sun came up the next morning, the king hurried to the lions' den. As he got close, the king called out to Daniel, asking if God was able to save him. Here's what Daniel said: "My God sent his angel, and he shut the mouths of the lions. They have not hurt me, because I was found innocent in his sight. Nor have I ever done any wrong before you" (6:22). The king was so excited. He had

Daniel lifted from the pit and saw that not even a scratch was on him.

The king ordered the men who had tried to get Daniel in trouble and their families to be thrown to the lions. And then he wrote a decree to all the people living around the world. The king wanted everyone to honor God. He wrote: "For he is the living God and he endures forever; his kingdom will not be destroyed, his dominion will never end. He rescues and he saves; he performs signs and wonders in the heavens and on the earth" (6:26–27).

6

A Dream of Four Beasts!

While Daniel was busy interpreting the dreams of kings, he himself was also having dreams. These can be very confusing and hard to understand, but the most important thing to remember is that God gave Daniel these dreams to give the people hope.

One dream that Daniel had was about four big beasts. These beasts represented four empires that each had control over the land that God's people lived in.

The dream began with Daniel standing on a beach, and the wind stirred up the waters. And then creatures emerged from the sea. The first beast to appear looked like a lion but had wings like an eagle. As Daniel continued to watch, the lion was lifted up as the wings were removed. The

creature stood on two feet like a man, and Daniel saw a man's mind was given to the lion.

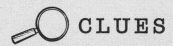

The next beast that appeared looked like a bear. Daniel saw three ribs in its mouth. A voice commanded the bear to eat until it was satisfied. The third creature that appeared before Daniel resembled a leopard. It had four wings on its back. This animal had four heads and "was given authority to rule" (7:6). The last creature appeared at night and was very powerful. Daniel described it as "terrifying and frightening" (v. 7). It had large teeth made of iron, and it destroyed everything in sight. It was different from all the

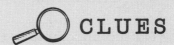

CLUES

The beast that looked like a bear represented the Persian Empire, and the ribs symbolized the lands that it had conquered.

other beasts and had ten horns. All these creatures were eventually destroyed. Daniel recorded these dreams as a way to give the people of God hope. He was saying that we may face hard times now, but as a part of God's kingdom, we cannot be defeated!

The dream ended with Daniel seeing a figure he called "one like a son of man, coming with the clouds of heaven.... He was given authority, glory and sovereign power" (7:13–14). Daniel asked someone next to him for help in understanding the dream. This was a reference to Jesus who came from

CLUES

The third beast represented the Greek Empire. This empire was greater than the "lion" in that it had four wings instead of the lion's two. The four heads represented the four captains who each received a portion of the empire after Alexander the Great died.

above, while the beasts came from below. The beasts represented kings who ruled for a short while, but God's children would receive the kingdom and live with Him forever in heaven. And for us today, this means, as we will see, that even though bad things happen, Jesus is our ultimate King, and He has already won the battle for our hearts.

 CLUES

Scholars believe the last creature symbolized either Rome or Syria. Both were empires and both brought suffering upon the people of God. The large teeth made of iron refer to the armies and the bad things they did. Daniel said that at this point, a small horn came up between them. It had a mouth and eyes and started to speak. Then the beast was destroyed and thrown into a fire, while the other three creatures were allowed to live for a while longer.

7

Daniel's Prayer

After his dreams, Daniel began thinking about how the city of Jerusalem would be destroyed and how the hard times would last seventy years. He was sad and went to the Lord in prayer. Daniel fasted and wore sackcloth too. Sackcloth was a rough material made from goat's hair—and it wasn't comfortable. In Bible times, people wore sackcloth as a sign of being sorry for something.

Daniel began his prayer by telling God that He was great and awesome and kept His promises. He said that God loves those who love Him and keep His commandments. Then Daniel admitted that his people had sinned. He said that everyone had rebelled and turned away from God's laws.

Daniel continued to pray, telling God that He

is righteous, but everyone is covered in shame. Daniel said that God is merciful and forgiving. Daniel cried out for God to hear his plea for help. "We do not make requests of you because we are righteous, but because of your great mercy" (9:18). Daniel's prayer turned his heart to God's as he begged God to help.

While Daniel was offering up this prayer, the angel Gabriel came to him again with a message of "seventy sevens." Gabriel told Daniel that while he was praying, word traveled out, and Gabriel received a message that Daniel was praying and went to him. Gabriel said, "Seventy 'sevens' are decreed for your people and your holy city to finish transgression, to put an end to sin, to atone for wickedness, to bring in everlasting righteousness, to seal up vision and prophecy and to anoint the Most Holy Place" (9:24).

The people ended their sinful ways, asked

forgiveness, returned to Jerusalem, and began again. The important part of this message is that Jesus is mentioned as the "Anointed One" (9:26). The message says He will be put to death and have nothing, but that in the end, His eternal and perfect kingdom will come.

Then Daniel had another vision of a man wearing linen and a belt of gold. His body was like topaz and his face like lightning. His eyes were like flaming torches, his arms and legs were like bronze, and his voice sounded like a great crowd. Daniel was learning that there were battles going on behind the scenes in unseen places. Through it all, God was working out His plans to help the people get back to their homeland in Israel.

More Visions of Kings

Daniel continued to have visions that helped him understand God's plan for His people. Daniel learned that there would be kings who would try to harm the Jewish people.

Daniel also learned about the "end times." Daniel heard about the great angel Michael who will rise up and protect God's people. The prophet was also told that believers will have everlasting life with God, but unbelievers will go to a separate place where they experience "shame and everlasting contempt" (12:2). Daniel also learned that "those who are wise

 **CLUES**

There will be difficult days, but in the end, Jesus is the victorious King who will save His people.

will shine like the brightness of the heavens, and those who lead many to righteousness, like the stars for ever and ever" (12:3).

There were parts of Daniel's visions that he did not completely understand, but he was told by the messenger, "Go your way till the end. You will rest, and then at the end of the days you will rise to receive your allotted inheritance" (12:13). That is how Daniel's story, as recorded in the Bible, ends. It ends on a promise that one day God would take Daniel home to heaven, and while Daniel waited for that day, he would have peace knowing that God is sovereign and would continue to take care of him.

9

Now that we've investigated the life of Daniel, it's time to think about some lessons we can learn from his story. A lot of Daniel's kingdom work involved using his wisdom to help the very people who held him captive. One of the common themes of Daniel's story is relying on God and staying connected to Him in many different ways. Daniel talked to God about everything, and he always listened to God's instructions. And not only did he listen, but he acted on what he knew was God's desire for his life.

Daniel's story was filled with stresses and successes. He had days when he wasn't sure what was going to happen to him and other days when he could see God at work. Whatever came his way, good or bad, Daniel stood up for God, because that was how he knew life should be lived—standing up for God, because that's what God deserves.

From the start, when Daniel and his people were taken hundreds of miles away to captivity, and until the end of his seventy years of ministry, the prophet took each step with full trust in God and His Word. Daniel didn't allow the day's events to control his view of God. Daniel didn't let his circumstances determine his feelings. Trusting his Creator to know what was best for his life took Daniel further than he ever could have gone if he had doubted.

Daniel learned how to trust God and be faithful. He kept God number one in his life.

Daniel didn't let fear of the unknown dictate his actions or moods. He persevered in a foreign place for seven decades because of his unfaltering faith in God. Daniel persevered because he knew with all his heart that God is in control of everything. God made everything. He is Lord of all, stronger than any force of evil and giver of every blessing. Daniel knew life made sense when he followed God instead of running out ahead of Him.

God also teaches us through Daniel's life that He has a purpose for everything. Life won't always be perfect and stress-free. And life won't always be the same for everyone. God makes His children special and doesn't want them to give up or compare their lives to the lives of other believers. God has a unique and special plan for each one of His children!

Daniel learned along the way that God is a mighty protector. He goes before us and isn't taken off guard by the hard things that come our way. He knows everything we're going through. And for everything you experience, God will use you to do great things for His kingdom and glory.

Now let's look at each one of these valuable lessons individually and some memory verses that will help plant God's truth in our hearts.

Power-Up #1:

MAKE PRAYER A HABIT.

Daniel's story is filled with times when he prayed. Making the right choices and reading the Bible are both very important, but prayer is like the glue that connects us to God. By using Daniel's prayers as examples, we can see that prayer isn't just asking God for things, but praising Him for who He is and what He's done for us. Whatever kind of day you're having, tell God all about it. Sharing your feelings will help keep things on the right track. Talking to God and making prayer a habit will help you know that, no matter what, God is right there listening.

Power-Up #2:

STAND UP FOR GOD.

Daniel stood strong for his heavenly Father. In the beginning of his story, Daniel had to make a very difficult decision about the kind of food he was going to eat. When he was offered food from the king's table, Daniel was tempted to change his ways and start heading down a path that would have him relying on the king's gifts. But Daniel knew better. As hard as it might have been, Daniel decided to rely on God instead. He had courage to tell the king's official that he wanted only vegetables and water. He wasn't worried about sounding ungrateful. Daniel only wanted to make sure the people he came in contact with knew that God was worth standing up for.

MEMORY VERSE: It is for freedom that Christ has set us free. Stand firm, then, and do not let yourselves be burdened again by a yoke of slavery. GALATIANS 5:1

Power-Up #3:
TRUST GOD.

When Daniel and his friends were taken captive, their future was uncertain. There were days when Daniel surely wondered what God's plan was in all of it. But through it all, Daniel continued to trust in God. He would end up ministering in his place of captivity for seventy years! At some point, Daniel knew in his heart that the kingdom work God had for him meant staying in the foreign land. Trusting in God wasn't easy. Remember,

Daniel trusted God and still wound up in a den of hungry lions. The important thing to know is that God made you special, and He won't let you go. He has a plan and knows what's best for you. Trust Him more and more as you grow in your faith and get closer to Him.

MEMORY VERSE: The LORD is my strength and my shield; my heart trusts in him, and he helps me. My heart leaps for joy, and with my song I praise him.
PSALM 28:7

Power-Up #4:

REMAIN FAITHFUL.

Daniel stayed connected to God through every trial because he knew that God cared about him. Daniel knew that God would be there for him through everything life would bring. Lives were changed because Daniel had faith in God's love and power. Whether it was food or prayer time, Daniel made it a priority to put God first. Being faithful to God means we pray for wisdom and strength to read our Bibles and let Him guide us in everything we do.

MEMORY VERSE: My eyes will be on the faithful in the land, that they may dwell with me. PSALM 101:6

Power-Up #5:
GOD IS IN CONTROL.

Daniel could have easily given in to fear when he was taken captive. He could have quickly decided to trust in himself and all the things he could see with his eyes. Daniel would have felt good too. Remember, the king offered him the best food and a comfortable life, but Daniel wanted something better. Daniel wanted a relationship with his Creator. For Daniel, God wasn't some unseen force but a Father and Friend. Daniel knew God's grace was enough to get him through every situation. God kept proving Himself faithful to Daniel, which made it easy for Daniel to constantly trust that God was in control of his life.

MEMORY VERSE: "So do not fear, for I am with you; do not be dismayed, for I am your God. I will strengthen you and help you; I will uphold you with my righteous right hand." ISAIAH 41:10

Power-Up #6:

GOD HAS A PURPOSE.

One of the inspirational traits of Daniel's character was his ability to always trust that God knows what He's doing. From the beginning, Daniel acted on faith, knowing that God had plans for his life. Daniel also knew that there was a very real enemy (the devil) trying to throw Daniel off track. He knew the enemy wanted to keep Daniel's eyes off God and on his situation. But Daniel stayed on the path God had for him, not wishing he was someplace else doing some other work. He trusted God's purposes, and he kept his heart and mind in God's truth.

MEMORY VERSE: "For I know the plans I have for you," declares the Lord, "plans to prosper you and not to harm you, plans to give you hope and a future." JEREMIAH 29:11

Power-Up #7:
DON'T QUIT.

Daniel knew how to keep going for God. He knew how to persevere through the tough times. He relied on God's unstoppable love as he ministered to the kings in Babylon. Daniel didn't give up on God, because he knew that God would never give up on him. Daniel kept his daily faith because he knew God is a promise keeper. Daniel always took God at His word and was blessed because of it.

MEMORY VERSE: Let us not become weary in doing good, for at the proper time we will reap a harvest if we do not give up. GALATIANS 6:9

Power-Up #8:
GOD PROTECTS.

Daniel's kingdom work teaches us that he lived and moved under God's protection. From the beginning, when his city was invaded, Daniel was protected by God. God wasn't taken by surprise when Nebuchadnezzar's men ransacked Jerusalem. God had Daniel covered both then and during the journey to Babylon. God continued to protect Daniel as he received an education. And when Nebuchadnezzar made everyone bow down to his gigantic statue, Daniel's friends refused to bow down, knowing God would protect them too. Daniel didn't worry about the results, because he was confident that God was his strength and shield.

MEMORY VERSE: But the Lord is faithful, and he will strengthen you and protect you from the evil one.
2 THESSALONIANS 3:3

Power-Up #9:
GOD KNOWS.

Daniel didn't let his circumstances determine his faith. He understood that God had a plan for his life and that nothing would happen to him without God knowing about it. God was with Daniel before he was taken into captivity, and He remained with him every moment after. When we really believe that God knows everything we're going through, then we can live boldly for Him.

When we trust that God sees and feels all our joy and all our sorrows, we find true comfort.

God made you and knows you, and He doesn't make mistakes, so follow Him always.

MEMORY VERSE: Great is our Lord and mighty in power; his understanding has no limit. PSALM 147:5

Power-Up #10:

GOD WILL USE YOU.

The same great and loving God who made
the universe carefully and lovingly made you!
Believe the truth that He loves you very much
and has great things planned for your life.
Daniel's life is an example that God's plans
and our plans might be totally different. So,
like Daniel, we just have to be available for
God to use us for His kingdom and His glory.

If we get into the habit of praying and asking God for His guidance, then we will step out in faith and leave the results up to Him. God will use you for His glory because He cares about you.

MEMORY VERSE: For it is God who works in you to will and to act in order to fulfill his good purpose. PHILIPPIANS 2:13

Kingdom Files:

Who Was Esther?

Dear Reading Detective,

Welcome to Kingdom Files! You're now a very important part of the Kingdom Files investigation—a series of really cool biographies all found in the Bible. Each case you investigate focuses on an important Bible character and is separated into three sections to make your time fun and interesting. First, you'll find the **Fact File**, which contains key information about a specific Bible character whom God called to do big things for His kingdom. Next, you'll read through an **Action File** that lays out Bible events showing the character in action. And finally, the **Power File** is where you'll find valuable information and memory verses to help you see how God is working in your life too. Along the way, **Clue Boxes** will offer applications to help you keep track of your thoughts as you make your way through the files. You can also use these sections to record questions you might have along Esther's journey. Write down any questions, and then ask your parents to get them involved in your quest.

Before you begin, know this: not only did God have plans for the Bible characters you'll read about in the Kingdom Files, but Jeremiah 29:11 says that God has big plans for you too! I pray that *Kingdom Files: Who Was Esther?* helps you get a bigger picture of God and that you will see just how much He loves you!

Blessings,
M.K.

Name: **ESTHER**

Occupation: **queen of Persia**

From: **Persia**

Years Active: **483–473 BC**

Kingdom Work: **served as a queen and helped save the lives of many people**

Key Stats:
+ The Jewish people are threatened by an evil plot.

+ Esther has the courage to stand up for her people.

+ The Jews are saved from destruction!

Mini Timeline:

538 BC
First exiles
return to
Jerusalem

486 BC
Xerxes
becomes
king of
Persia

479 BC
Esther
becomes
queen

A King, a Party, and a Queen

The book of Esther gives us hope that God cares all about our daily lives. Whether it's something personal that we struggle with like being anxious, or problems with other people like being bullied or feeling left out, studying Esther's story will encourage us to remember that God is in control and always on our side. It's a story of hope that reminds us that God is our Protector and He cares about all the things that we care about.

Our investigation into the life of Esther begins in a land called Persia in the year 483 BC. Persia was a place in the Middle East. If you find Iran on a world map, you will see where Persia was located. Persia covered so much land back in the time of Esther that it was known as an empire. To get an idea of how large Persia was, look back at the world map and find Greece. Now look right until you find India. All the land in between was Persia!

Esther's story starts with a king, a party, and a queen. Esther's parents were most likely a part of the people from Jerusalem who were exiled to Babylon under the rule of King Nebuchadnezzar. *Exiled* means people are forced to move far away from their homes. As was the case for Esther's parents, they were made to move to a foreign country that had a different culture and different language.

The book of Esther takes place 103 years after the Jewish people were taken captive and 54 years after a man named Zerubbabel led the first group of exiles back from Persia to their homeland in Jerusalem.

The Persian king, Cyrus, said that the captives could return to Jerusalem; however, many of the Jewish people decided to stay in Persia. Esther's parents were part of the group that did not want to return to their homeland.

Esther's story takes place in a nation called Persia and Media. This was the most powerful nation in the world at the time. A proud king named Xerxes was in charge of this massive kingdom that stretched all the way from Ethiopia to

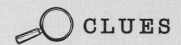

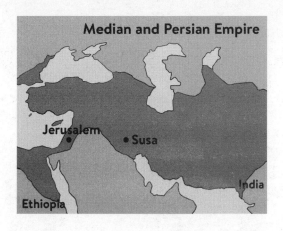

India—127 provinces in all. While there were palaces all over the land, a very large one was located at a place called Susa. Xerxes wanted to throw a big party for all his officials and leaders so he could show off everything that he had accomplished.

Xerxes was very rich and liked to have fun, so he decided to make the party last for 180 days! This six-month

 CLUES

Xerxes was most likely trying to show off in front of military leaders so they would want to join his army.

festival would show off how glorious his kingdom was. The Bible tells us that after that huge party was over, the king hosted another party that lasted for seven days. This second party was for all the people who lived in the city. No matter if they were rich or poor, the king invited them in, and they all were served in the gardens. This was a beautiful display of the king's money and power. The people sat on couches made of gold and silver and drank from golden cups. White and blue linens hung from marble pillars all around the garden. The king made sure everyone received the royal treatment!

The queen at that time was Vashti, and she liked to throw parties too. The Bible says that while all the king's festivities were happening, Vashti was hosting a banquet for the women in the palace. It was customary for women not to appear in public, so the queen had her own gathering for the ladies.

The king sent his men to bring his queen to the

party so he could show everyone how beautiful she was. But the queen refused to go! No one knows why she refused, but this was where all the weeks of fun came to an abrupt end. Vashti did not do as the king ordered, so "the king became furious and burned with anger" (1:12). And even though Esther hasn't been mentioned in the story yet, this scene sets up the reason she was called out of her everyday life and into God's kingdom work!

Xerxes summoned all the people who were closest to him, his advisers, and asked what he should do. They all said he should punish Vashti because if she wouldn't obey the king, then all the other noblewomen in the kingdom might act in the same way. That sounds silly, but way back then, things were different. The biggest responsibility the advisers had was to make sure no one disrespected the king! King Xerxes needed

to act quickly, and that's exactly what he did.

The first royal decree was sent out: Vashti was not allowed in the king's presence. She was no longer the queen. Her behavior didn't please the king, so a new queen would need to be found. And just like that, Vashti was out. The king made another order. A second decree went out: "Every man should be ruler over his own household" (1:22). At that time, a royal decree could not be undone. Vashti could never be queen again.

God was using this very unfortunate situation to make a way for Esther to enter into the king's palace.

2

A New Queen

Four long years passed between Vashti's re-
moval as queen and Esther's arrival. The king
and his army had battled against
Greece. Back in Bible times,
there were a lot of bat-
tles fought to gain
or keep control of
land. The Persian
Empire covered so
much land that Xerxes,
as king, had to fight many
battles to keep his rule
strong. He was not successful, and so the king was
back in the palace,

defeated and all alone. King Xerxes thought about Vashti, but because of the royal order he had given, she could not come back.

The king's servants came to Xerxes and told him to order a search

CLUES

God was not far away. He was using Vashti's dismissal as a way to eventually protect His people.

for a new queen. Xerxes liked this idea, so word was sent throughout the kingdom. This is where Esther came into the picture. She had an older cousin named Mordecai. Mordecai was a man who lived in the Persian city of Susa. He most likely worked for the king because of his position at the city gate. Seeing that

Esther had been orphaned, Mordecai adopted and raised Esther "as his own daughter when her father and mother died" (2:7). At some time during the search for a new queen, Esther was brought to the palace.

Esther was part of a group of young women taken from their everyday lives and brought to the king's castle. One day she was doing her normal routine—drawing water from a well, playing games, and buying vegetables at the local market—and the next she was being whisked away by the king's soldiers. Esther must have been anxious and unsure about her future, but she trusted God. This was also hard for Esther, because she was taken from her only relative. Away from Mordecai, the only family she had left, Esther was escorted to the castle and forced to grow up in a hurry. She was surely confused about her new position, but Esther never stopped believing that God was in charge of her life.

At the palace, Esther immediately found favor with a man named Hegai, who was in charge of finding the next queen. Esther even received "beauty treatments and special food" (2:9). While all this was happening, Esther did not tell anyone that she was Jewish. Mordecai had instructed her not to say anything about her background. He had a feeling that things wouldn't go well if the king and his assembly knew Esther was Jewish.

 **CLUES**

Esther's Hebrew name was Hadassah, which means "myrtle," but her Persian name was Esther.

Esther respected her cousin's wishes and kept her identity a secret.

While all this beauty work was going on, Mordecai stuck close to the palace courtyard where Esther was so he would know how she was doing. He wanted to make sure no harm came her way. Mordecai showed that he was a loyal man by caring for Esther.

For one whole year, Esther and the other women went through a process of beauty treatments to look nice: "six months with oil of myrrh and six with perfumes and cosmetics" (2:12). The Bible says that Esther won the favor of everyone who saw her, even the king.

On the surface, Esther's story is very similar to our spiritual life stories because she was taken from a faraway place into the presence of a king, just as Jesus saves us from our sins and brings us into His Father's house!

3

A Conspiracy and a Very Bad Plan

After many days of training and preparing, the time had come for Esther to go to the king. Standing in the royal palace, she soon learned that the king liked her more than any of the other young ladies he had seen. Xerxes took the royal crown and placed it on Esther's head. This act made her the queen of the whole land of Persia!

A while later, Mordecai was again at the king's gate keeping watch and overheard two

CLUES

You can see God orchestrating events so that Esther will be seen in an even bigger and better light.

of the king's officials, Bigthana and Teresh, talking about an evil plan. The men were scheming to take Xerxes' life. Mordecai knew what had to be done. He told Queen Esther, "who in turn reported it to the king, giving credit to Mordecai" (2:22). Because of Mordecai's quick thinking, the king was safe.

Things were going well for Xerxes. He had a new queen, and his empire was still the largest in the land. Sometime later the king promoted a man named Haman to a seat of special honor that put him in a very high position over all the other nobles. The king called for all the royal officials to kneel before Haman at the city gate. Remember, Mordecai held a position in the king's court, but

he refused to obey the rule and would not bow to Haman. This was because Mordecai obeyed God. He had the courage not to give in to the king's order.

The royal officials saw that Mordecai refused to bow to Haman and questioned him about it. "Day after day they spoke to him but he refused to comply" (3:4). The men took the report back to

Haman, who became furious when he saw that Mordecai would not honor him. Haman was in a position of authority. When he heard that Mordecai was a Jew, he wanted to find a way to destroy not only Mordecai but all the Jewish people "throughout the whole kingdom of Xerxes" (3:6).

Haman found himself in the company of the king and told him all about Mordecai's disrespect and the others who did not do as they were told. "Their customs are different from those of all other people, and they do not obey the king's laws; it is not in the king's best interest to tolerate them" (3:8). This was exactly what Mordecai was trying to warn Esther about. Esther was about to face a very big problem that would require great courage on her part. Haman wanted to do away with the Jewish people, and Mordecai knew that the king would more than likely sign a decree to help Haman accomplish his evil plan.

Xerxes agreed with Haman and even told him he could attack the Jewish people. The king took off his signet ring and gave it to Haman. Orders would be written up so that Jewish people in every province across the kingdom would be under attack. The king's ring would be used to seal the orders so the people would know the orders were officially from the king. Xerxes gave his chief official full authority to do great harm to Esther's people. All because Mordecai refused to kneel before Haman.

Remember. . .Queen Esther was Jewish too!

The plan that Haman tried to carry out was very evil. Haman wanted to take the lives of all the Jews who lived all throughout the king's realm. His plan was publicized everywhere. This

terrible moment was one that God wouldn't stand
for. Even though the situation looked bleak, God
was at work behind the scenes.

4

Mordecai Asks Esther to Help

When Mordecai heard of Haman's plan, he was very sad. "He tore his clothes, put on sackcloth and ashes, and went out into the city, wailing loudly and bitterly" (4:1). The situation seemed hopeless, and Mordecai couldn't contain his emotions. He must have felt responsible for the threat that was now against the Jews. Things just kept getting worse, and Mordecai couldn't see how the situation would ever change.

People couldn't help but wonder about the grown man who was tearing his clothes in the middle of the street and wailing. They stopped and stared at the man covered in ashes and sackcloth. Some of them knew that Mordecai and Esther were related, and they sent word about Mordecai's actions back to Esther. She had clothes sent to him, but he refused to put them on. Wearing sackcloth was a sign of seeking forgiveness and humbling oneself before God. And Mordecai knew the only way out of this situation would be through the power of God.

Esther sent one of her helpers to find Mordecai to see what was bothering him. Hathak went out and listened as Mordecai retold all the terrible things that Haman planned to do to the Jewish people. Mordecai asked Hathak to have

Esther go to the king and "beg for mercy and plead with him for her people" (4:8).

Esther was concerned because Mordecai's request would put her in a very dangerous position. Anyone who approached the king uninvited, including the queen, would be severely punished. She told Hathak to go back to Mordecai and tell him that anyone who went to the king without being summoned would be put to death, unless the king extended the gold scepter to them and spared their life.

Mordecai had a sobering reply for the queen: "Do not think that because you are in the king's house you alone of all the Jews will escape" (4:13). Mordecai wasn't about to give up trying to get Esther to see how serious the situation was. He went on to tell her that if she didn't do anything to help, the Jewish people would receive deliverance from another place. This means that

God would protect His people. If Esther didn't act to help the situation, God would still keep His word because He is a promise keeper.

Esther knew that the time had come to make a choice. She didn't waste a moment. The queen instructed Mordecai to gather all the Jews who lived in the region and have them fast—not eat or drink anything—for three days. Esther added that she too would do the same

 **CLUES**

Mordecai knew it was time for Esther to put her complete trust in God. It wasn't going to be easy, but it was what she had to do.

thing. She promised Mordecai that after her fasting period was done, she would go to the king, "even though it is against the law. And if I perish, I perish" (4:16). Esther was willing to risk her own life for the sake of all her people. She was willing to put others above herself.

Esther is a great example of submitting to God even in very difficult times.

 **CLUES**

Fasting is a common practice all throughout the Bible. Jesus even fasted for a very long time to be able to focus on God's will for His life. Fasting helped a person rely on God instead of relying on things of the world.

5

Esther's Plan

Esther had the courage to be a woman of her word. Remember, she was queen! In terms of money and comfort, Esther was all set. She didn't need anything. But in her heart, she knew that Mordecai was right. God had brought her to this position of influence for a very important reason. Her people were depending on her. After fasting for three whole days, Esther mustered up the faith it took to stand before the king, knowing that God was on her side.

Esther was ready to go to Xerxes and confront him about Haman's terrible idea. But first she needed to gain the king's trust before she would reveal the evil plot. She went to the king's hall and waited to speak to Xerxes.

He asked what she needed and said, "Even up to half the kingdom, it will be given you" (5:3). Esther's plan included inviting the king and Haman to a banquet that she personally prepared. She wanted them to let their guards down and be happy. The king quickly accepted her invitation. "Bring Haman at once. . .so that we may do what Esther asks" (5:5).

At the banquet, the king and Haman were present, enjoying the meal that Esther had prepared for them. Xerxes, again, asked Esther what she wanted: "Now what is your petition? It will be given you. And what is your request? Even up to half the kingdom, it will be granted"

CLUES

Esther is a great role model because she didn't let fear stop her from doing the right thing. She trusted that God was big enough to handle her problems. Knowing that truth, she stepped out in faith and acted.

(5:6). Esther thought about it, but she knew the time wasn't right to discuss the situation with the king. She wasn't going to back down, but she was going to wait on God's timing. Another invitation had to come first. Esther replied to the king with another offer. She invited the king to bring Haman to a second banquet the following day. She would prepare another extraordinary dining experience. After she invited them, Esther said, "Then I will answer the king's question" (5:8).

Twice Esther waited to give her specific request that the king protect her people. The whole time they enjoyed the wide variety of food and drink, Esther was preparing to take her request to the king. Don't forget she had fasted to make sure things were right between her and God. Waiting on God's perfect timing was something Esther was trying hard to do.

Meanwhile, Haman was out walking and was "happy and in high spirits" (5:9). He thought it was wonderful to be treated with such respect. He felt proud to be honored with all these fancy meals. What a feast he enjoyed at the favor of Queen Esther! If she put together such an awesome meal for him, all the officials he would come in contact with should surely bow to him and treat him with the same respect. That's when he came across Mordecai at the king's gate.

This time Haman was determined that

Mordecai would bow. However, yet again, Mordecai didn't bow or show fear toward Haman. This greatly angered the king's official. The Bible says that Haman was filled with rage—intense anger—against Mordecai but restrained himself and went home (5:9–10). Haman was really mad at Mordecai, but he controlled his feelings and  didn't say anything to him.

Haman was rather selfish, and when he arrived home, he called his friends and his wife, Zeresh, and began boasting to them about his wealth and his many children. This was a man who liked the way things looked on the outside but didn't care about what was on the inside.

Mordecai had irritated him by not bowing to him. To Haman, that was very disrespectful. Haman bragged to his wife and friends so he could feel good about himself.

He was also very happy to announce that the king had "elevated him above the other nobles and officials" (5:11). This was a very proud moment for the king's highest official. He had been invited to a private banquet with the king and queen and elevated to a high-ranking position in the king's court. This was his time to shine. Haman believed that all these titles and connections made him more important than he really was.

Haman was not at a loss for finding ways to praise himself. He went on to tell his friends that he was the only person Queen Esther invited along with the king to the banquet. But then Haman admitted that even with all those gifts, he was still angry and depressed because he kept seeing Mordecai at the king's gate. He told his family and friends that the man always refused to bow down to him. This was unacceptable to Haman, and he wanted something to be done to teach Mordecai a lesson.

After she listened to her husband's complaints, Haman's wife had an answer. She gave her husband an idea to set up a pole that was roughly seventy-five feet tall. This would become a thing called a gallows. The gallows were used in Bible times as a punishment to hang someone who had committed a crime. The gallows had two poles connected by a cross bar. From the cross bar, there would hang a rope. Haman's wife said that she wanted Mordecai to die on the gallows. Zeresh told her husband to go to the king and share their idea. She figured that if this man Mordecai was such a problem for her husband, then he should be done away with. Haman listened to his wife and had the pole set up. Then he went to the banquet with King Xerxes, excited to share his wife's idea.

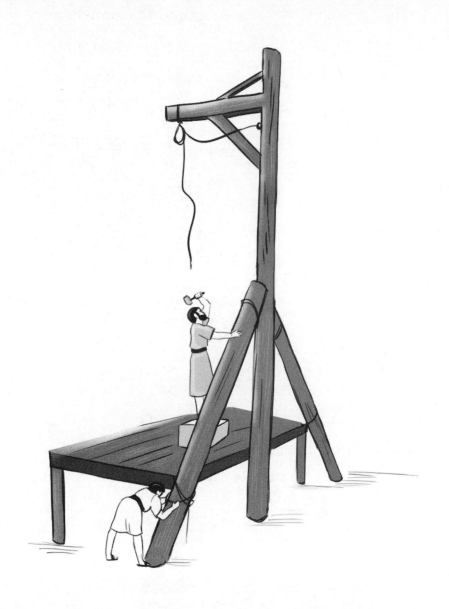

6

What Happened Next

The Bible says that the king couldn't sleep, so he had his people bring the book of chronicles to him and read it out loud. The chronicles were

books of history. As he listened to all the accomplishments of his people and his empire, Xerxes learned about how Mordecai uncovered the officials' plot to take the life of the king. Xerxes couldn't believe it. He asked what special honor had been given to Mordecai for his bravery in saving the king's life. "Nothing has been done for him," was the answer (6:3).

The king asked who was there in the court to help honor Mordecai. Now, while all this was going on, Haman entered the court to tell the king about his new evil plan to kill Mordecai. Xerxes ordered Haman to be brought in. From Haman's view, it was good news that the king was going to hear about his plan to do away with Mordecai.

The king asked Haman what should be done for a person he wanted to honor. Haman thought Xerxes was talking about him, so he said the person deserved to wear one of the king's royal robes and ride on one of the king's horses through the city. Haman's selfish pride was growing. He couldn't be happier. His king was about to reward him in a big way!

The king liked what Haman had suggested and ordered him to go and get the things he mentioned. Haman obeyed. Can you picture the pride growing inside Haman? Can you picture the smile on his face as he went to get the piece of clothing that would make him look like royalty? Haman collected the royal robe and one of the king's horses and brought them both back to the king. It was almost time to wear the robe and ride around on the king's horse, having everyone give him praise.

King Xerxes then told Haman news that he never would have imagined the king would tell him. Haman's mouth must have dropped open when Xerxes said that all of those things were for Mordecai. The Bible says Haman "robed Mordecai, and led him on horseback through the city streets" (6:11).

After the humiliating experience of having to

shower praise on Mordecai, Haman raced home
and told his wife the bad news. His wife and
friends warned him that it wouldn't be a good
idea to stand in Mordecai's way. Haman was
confused. But there was still the banquet. . .
Things weren't all that bad.

The king's men soon came to take Haman to
the banquet Esther had invited him to. He had
been humiliated, and now it was time to go back

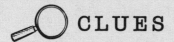

CLUES

Can you imagine? First, Haman was trying to harm Mordecai, but now he was being made to parade the man around to gain honor from the people. Haman had to watch his enemy get the praise that he wanted for himself. Surely Mordecai couldn't believe it either!

to the king. Haman's life was a mess, and he hoped that something would change for the better—and soon.

7

Haman's Fate

At the banquet, the king again asked Esther what it was that she wanted. The time had come for Esther to stick up for what was right. She told Xerxes that what she wanted more than anything was for her people to be spared. This is when she made the big announcement. Esther was about to speak the one thing that Mordecai told her not to speak. Queen Esther told the king that she too was Jewish. "For I and my people have been sold to be destroyed" (7:4).

Right there at table, the king asked Esther who the person was behind all these accusations, and she said, "An adversary and enemy! This vile Haman!" (7:6).

Right then Haman was very afraid. Not only

was he not receiving the praise he desired, but now Esther had told the king about his plan.

King Xerxes was so mad that he got up from the table and went outside to the palace gardens. Haman knew that his life was in danger, so he stayed with Esther, asking her to spare his life. The Bible says that he sat on her couch begging her. Meanwhile, the king came back in from the gardens and saw Haman talking with Esther.

Xerxes thought Haman was trying to hurt his

queen. To make matters worse, one of the king's helpers took the opportunity to tell Xerxes about the gallows that Haman had built to kill Mordecai. The king was furious and ordered Haman's life to be taken on the same pole instead. Afterward, the Bible says that "the king's fury subsided" (7:10).

On the same day, the king gave Queen Esther all of Haman's estate. Xerxes also invited Mordecai to come into his presence because Esther had told the king how they were related. Then the king gave Mordecai his signet ring, and Esther appointed Mordecai to be in charge of Haman's estate. What a turn of events! Everything that Haman had wanted was given to Mordecai.

Esther again pleaded with Xerxes so that he would stop the evil plan Haman had created to destroy the Jewish people. "Let an order be written overruling the dispatches that Haman... devised and wrote to destroy the Jews in all the king's provinces" (8:5). The king gave Mordecai permission to write a letter that gave the Jews permission to arm themselves and defend their families. This meant that they were now protected under order of the king. The order was posted in public places "so that the Jews would be ready on that day to avenge themselves on their enemies" (8:13).

Esther's boldness resulted in salvation for her

people. She refused to let evil intimidate her. Her courage to approach the king with the request for Xerxes to protect her people resulted in the saving of many lives. "For the Jews it was a time of happiness and joy, gladness and honor" (8:16).

Because of God's faithfulness and Esther's desire to serve her Creator, all the Jewish people were defended and saved.

8

In the End

God used Mordecai to help take care of and protect Esther, just like He used Esther to help take care of and protect the Jewish people. The Bible says that Mordecai became more powerful and well known throughout the kingdom. His reputation spread across the land, and people were careful to do what he said. He and all the nobles helped the Jewish people strike down those who were trying to harm them. "The tables were turned and the Jews got the upper hand over those who hated them" (9:1).

Through Esther, God delivered the Jewish people and gave them victory over their enemies. "Their sorrow was turned into joy and their mourning into a day of celebration" (9:22).

Purim is still celebrated today with the reading of

CLUES

The modern-day Feast of Lots, called Purim, was started to celebrate God's faithfulness to deliver the Jewish people. Because Esther stood up for what was right, the Jewish people were saved. This is similar to what Jesus has done for all of us. Just like the Jewish people were about to face death at the hands of Xerxes' original order, all of us deserve to die because of our sins. But because of what Jesus did on the cross, we have been given the offer of eternal life.

the book of Esther. It is called the Feast of Lots, because Haman cast lots to determine the day that the Jews would be destroyed (9:24).

The book of Esther notes that Mordecai

became the second-highest-ranking official behind the king. He was well respected because he "worked for the good of his people and spoke up for the welfare of all the Jews" (10:3).

Things changed for Esther and Mordecai. They went from being alone to being heroes in God's epic plan. They no longer lived in fear because of their culture. They had obeyed God and followed His commands. Things weren't always easy, but they didn't have time to complain. They both knew that God's ways are always the best!

Now that we've investigated Esther's story, it's time to think about some lessons we can learn from her life. All the way from orphan to queen, Esther did a lot of great kingdom work for the Lord.

Esther made sure that God was the most important thing in her life. She gathered the courage from Him to speak up for what was right—and in doing so, she saved her people.

God made your life very special too, and He has a wonderful story that He's using you to write. It's a story that will lead others to the good news of Jesus!

Let's look at each one of these valuable lessons individually along with some memory verses that will help plant God's truth in our hearts.

Power-Up #1:

GOD IS ALWAYS WITH US.

Esther was an orphan, but just because she surely felt alone without her mother and father, that didn't mean God had abandoned her. He *never* abandons His people. Esther had faith in the promises of her heavenly Father. This gave her the courage to stand up to her enemy and trust that God had her back.

God was with Esther and delivered her and her people from the wickedness of Haman's hatred. Esther knew that it was important to trust that God was always with her and not doubt His eternal goodness. When the time came for Esther to make big decisions, she did not shy away in fear. Be encouraged by the fact that you are very important to God, and know that He is using you to do great things.

MEMORY VERSE: "The LORD your God is with you, the Mighty Warrior who saves. He will take great delight in you." ZEPHANIAH 3:17

Power-Up #2:
YOU MATTER.

You were created for a very special purpose. The God of the universe thought about you, and your life was made to glorify Him and reflect His goodness in a hurting world. It didn't matter what Esther's background was. It didn't matter that she was different from the people around her. She put her faith in the promises of God and gave the outcome of her life to Him. It's important to learn this lesson as you follow God. No matter what grade you're in, no matter how much money your family has or doesn't have, never forget that you matter to God.

Just like Esther found herself in the role of queen, she knew that she could never have gotten there without God's help.

That's the cool thing about Esther's story. She didn't wake up one day and wish to become married to the king of the greatest kingdom on earth. Esther simply made the most of every situation she was in and left the results to God. She didn't find her self-worth in material possessions or in the words of others. Esther put her trust in what God said about her! Living from that perspective helped Esther have the strength to stand up for what was right and save her people.

MEMORY VERSE: For you created my inmost being; you knit me together in my mother's womb. I praise you because I am fearfully and wonderfully made. PSALM 139:13–14

Power-Up #3:
GOD DELIVERS.

Esther knew that she couldn't convince the king without God's help. She had to act on truth but understood that any power she had as queen was given to her not by Xerxes but by God. Esther couldn't live each day in fear of the unknown but rather in faith that God would bring her to all the people and places that He wanted her to meet and see. She knew that God was with her everywhere she went.

God loves you and is with you through all the ups and downs of life. God isn't there just on the good days. Be confident, like Esther, that God is your Deliverer, all the time.

Power-Up #4:

DON'T LET FEAR
KEEP YOU FROM GOD.

There were plenty of times in Esther's life when she could have let fear stop her. When Mordecai told her about Haman's terrible plan, Esther knew it would take courage to approach the king. Her one bold decision to move forward with God's guidance and ask the king for help saved so many people. When fear creeps in, putting faith in God is the key. Overcome the struggles by trusting in God, who loves you more than anything. Haman was a grown-up bully, and Esther could have let fear keep her from standing up to him. Thankfully, she put her trust in God.

Remember that fear doesn't always come from other people. Sometimes it might come from inside us—in our thoughts, for example. That's when we have to act like Esther and rely on God's truth. We constantly have to read our Bibles and get help from other believers as we learn how to overcome fear.

MEMORY VERSE: When I am afraid, I put my trust in you. PSALM 56:3

Power-Up #5:
BE HUMBLE.

Sometimes it's hard to do the right thing. Sometimes it's hard to be patient and love other people when they act unlovable. Esther is a good role model in humility. At every turn, we read that she was finding favor with all the people in her life. She respected the wishes of Mordecai when he told her not to mention her heritage, and she kept that humble spirit all the way through the process of becoming queen. Like Esther, we should make it our goal to act in gentleness and love no matter what situation we're in.

Finding your value in who God says you are really makes all the difference. Knowing that you are a child of the King helps keep your heart filled with His eternal love. Esther understood this. The Bible says that she was very pretty, but that wasn't where her courage came from. When Mordecai told Esther not to mention her background, she humbly obeyed. Even when she became queen, Esther still honored Mordecai's request. She waited until the right time before taking action. Esther didn't jump ahead of God's plan.

MEMORY VERSE: Be completely humble and gentle; be patient, bearing with one another in love. EPHESIANS 4:2

Power-Up #6:
STAND UP FOR WHAT'S RIGHT.

Sometimes it's easier to avoid making hard choices. Maybe you know someone at school who is getting picked on or doesn't have any friends. We can learn from Esther's life that standing up for what's right may not be easy, but it's necessary. God was always with Esther, just like He's always with us. When the time came for Esther to approach the king for help in protecting her people, she stood up for what was right and didn't back down. This part of Esther's story shows that even if a choice is hard to make, if it's the right one, then make it—knowing that God is the One giving you the strength you need to succeed.

Who knows what would have happened if Esther hadn't stood up for her people? Most likely, things would have been very bad. Haman, after all, was a very evil person. Like Esther, we need to always be ready to do the right thing that honors God and helps protect and care for others.

MEMORY VERSE: And whatever you do, whether in word or deed, do it all in the name of the Lord Jesus, giving thanks to God the Father through him. COLOSSIANS 3:17

Power-Up #7:
BE WISE.

Being wise will help us connect with God. Esther was wise because she kept herself living daily life in a humble way. She learned to listen and take instructions from others. She didn't become selfish and only want her way of doing things. She learned to submit her will to the Lord and simply obey God.

God kept opening all the right doors for Esther, and she eventually became queen. She connected with God as she lived her life making wise decisions. For example, a wise decision is to do your homework and do it well. But sometimes you may not want to do it. Being wise in this situation will help you stay committed to your schoolwork, and you will be a better student because of it. Esther also gained wisdom by listening. She listened to Mordecai and was willing to risk her own safety because she knew what was true. Esther was wise in how she interacted with the king. She respected his position but wasn't afraid to speak truth. She used wisdom to make smart decisions that ultimately saved many lives.

MEMORY VERSE: "Therefore everyone who hears these words of mine and puts them into practice is like a wise man who built his house on the rock." MATTHEW 7:24

Power-Up #8:

TREAT OTHERS WITH RESPECT.

Esther decided that being obedient to God was a smart choice. She understood how important it is to live unselfishly by thinking about other people. Esther knew that the way she treated other people mattered. Esther understood that other people were created by God too and that she had to believe that the way she treated them was the way she was treating God.

When she was in the royal palace being taken care of and given special things, Esther still listened to Mordecai and respected his wishes not to mention her background.

Later, when Mordecai told her she needed to go to the king to save her people, Esther asked for prayer and said she would be fasting and praying too. Esther knew many things would compete for her attention and cause her to want to be selfish, but ultimately she had peace knowing that God was showing her how to serve others.

MEMORY VERSE: "Truly I tell you, whatever you did not do for one of the least of these, you did not do for me." MATTHEW 25:45

Power-Up #9:
BE COURAGEOUS.

Esther knew that God was in control of her life and the lives of her people. Still, she knew she had to act when it came time for her to help her people. Esther stepped out in courage even when she thought that approaching King Xerxes may have meant she'd lose her life. Being a part of God's kingdom work means being courageous in the face of hard times. God is the Creator. He made you to do things. He gave you a purpose. Rely on Him today, and go with courage to do great things for His glory. You are not alone. In God you are powerful and loved.

Sometimes things will happen that might make you feel insecure and weak. You might feel like you can't make a difference or help somebody. The truth is, with God's help, you can be a courageous person who cares for others, just like Esther cared. You can stand up and help someone know that they matter too. Throughout the Bible, God gives us the command to be strong and take courage. Take your courage from God as you wait on Him to direct your path.

MEMORY VERSE: For the Spirit God gave us does not make us timid, but gives us power, love and self-discipline. 2 TIMOTHY 1:7

Power-Up #10:
GOD IS BIGGER THAN
OUR PROBLEMS.

Just like Esther, we have problems. Everyone does. But Esther saw God as big and mighty, in control over everything, including her problems. Esther didn't let her problems overwhelm her. She kept her faith in God, knowing that the One who is all-powerful is bigger than the stressful times. Esther kept her eyes on God as she confronted the difficult times in her life.

What is it that you're worried about? What is that one problem in your life that seems to keep you down? Please don't forget that God is infinitely more powerful than anything. Have faith, like Esther, that God will never let you go or let you down.

Esther knew that God made her and loved her— not because Esther was queen, not because she was married to a powerful king, and not because of the size of the king's army. Esther knew that God alone could and would create a way through life's problems. She just had to stay connected to Him, and we need to do the same!

Esther found all her hope in God. That way she wouldn't be let down. Picture God standing between you and the problems you are facing.

MEMORY VERSE: "Ah, Sovereign LORD, you have made the heavens and the earth by your great power and outstretched arm. Nothing is too hard for you." JEREMIAH 32:17

Kingdom Files:

Who Was Mary, Mother of Jesus?

Dear Reading Detective,

Welcome to Kingdom Files! You're now a very important part of the Kingdom Files investigation—a series of really cool biographies all found in the Bible. Each case you investigate focuses on an important Bible character and is separated into three sections to make your time fun and interesting. First, you'll find the **Fact File**, which contains key information about a specific Bible character whom God called to do big things for His kingdom. Next, you'll read through an **Action File** that lays out Bible events showing the character in action. And finally, the **Power File** is where you'll find valuable information and memory verses to help you see how God is working in your life too. Along the way, **Clue Boxes** will offer applications to help you keep track of your thoughts as you make your way through the files. You can also use these sections to record questions you might have along Mary's journey. Write down any questions, and then ask your parents to get them involved in your quest.

Before you begin, know this: not only did God have plans for the Bible characters you'll read about in the Kingdom Files, but Jeremiah 29:11 says that God has big plans for you too! I pray that *Kingdom Files: Who Was Mary, Mother of Jesus?* helps you get a bigger picture of God and that you will see just how much He loves you!

Blessings,

M.K.

Name: **MARY**

Occupation: **mother of Jesus**

From: **Nazareth**

Years Active: **around 5 BC–AD 33**

Kingdom Work: **raised Jesus
and protected Him from Herod;
followed Jesus' teachings;
prayed for God's will to be done**

Key Stats:

✦ Gave birth to
Jesus

✦ Obeyed His
teachings

✦ Prayed with
other believers
for the Holy
Spirit

Mini Timeline:

5 BC	**2 BC**	**AD 12**	**AD 27**	**AD 31**
Gives birth to Jesus	Flees to Egypt	Finds Jesus in temple	Wedding at Cana	Witnesses Jesus' crucifixion

1

Great News!

Mary played a very special part in God's kingdom work. She was the young woman God chose to be the mother of Jesus! Her world was about to be turned upside down in a miraculous way.

A long time before Mary became pregnant, the prophet Isaiah talked about this special moment in history. This moment was special because God had chosen to send His only Son, Jesus, to be born of a virgin. It was so special because He was sending His only Son to take on flesh and become the Savior of the world. The prophet said that Mary would give birth to a son and name him Immanuel, which means "God with us" (Isaiah 7:14; Matthew 1:23).

An angel named Gabriel visited Mary in her
hometown of Nazareth in Galilee. This small

town was twelve miles south of the Sea of Galilee, situated on a high hill far away from the main roads. Nazareth held to strong Jewish traditions. It had a tiny population of less than five hundred people. The Nazarenes were farmers who raised livestock and planted orchards. The people spoke a language called Aramaic.

Gabriel said, "Greetings, you who are highly favored! The Lord is with you" (Luke 1:28). Mary was young (most likely not older than fifteen), and she was overwhelmed at the angel's words. Mary didn't understand the angel's message. Out of all the girls in the world at that time, God chose her for a very unique role. The angel went on to comfort Mary and remind her that she didn't need to be afraid. The angel said this about Jesus: "He will be great and will be called the Son of the Most High.... His kingdom will never end" (Luke 1:32–33).

Even though Mary didn't understand everything that was happening, she told the angel that she was the Lord's servant. She said, "May your word to me be fulfilled" (Luke 1:38). This gives us a good understanding of her relationship with God and her strong faith. Mary was pledged to wed a man named Joseph. Before they were actually married, a miracle happened and Mary was "found to be pregnant through the Holy Spirit" (Matthew 1:18).

This was a very stressful time for Mary, because in the culture of Mary's day, people wouldn't have understood what really happened. They would have judged her. Can you imagine all the stares and weird looks Mary must have received because of her pregnancy? And then when people would ask her to explain, Mary would begin her story with an angel appearing to her. That would surely have made people roll their eyes. Mary must have felt alone and afraid.

Joseph didn't want to bring any disgrace to Mary, so "he had in mind to divorce her quietly" (Matthew 1:19). That's when an angel appeared to

Joseph in a dream and told him not to be afraid to take Mary as his wife. The angel went on to explain that something very miraculous had happened

and that the baby inside Mary's belly was conceived from the Holy Spirit (Matthew 1:20). The angel also told Joseph that they were to name the baby Jesus because He was going to save people from their sins! After this message from the angel, Joseph and Mary became husband and wife.

At this time, Mary had a family member named Elizabeth who lived far away in a land called Judea. Mary left Nazareth and traveled the long distance to Judea after receiving news from the angel about her pregnancy. This escape to the hills would at least help Mary endure the first few months of her pregnancy away from curious villagers who wouldn't understand or believe her story.

When Mary arrived at her relative's house, she received

some really amazing news. Elizabeth was also pregnant! Her child was John the Baptist, who would be the one to share the good news of Jesus, the Messiah.

When Mary arrived at the door and greeted Elizabeth, the baby in Elizabeth's womb leaped for joy! Elizabeth immediately understood what had happened to Mary. She said to her, "Blessed are you among women, and blessed is the child you will bear!" (Luke 1:42). This helped Mary to know even more that she really was being used by God in a special way. Remember that Mary was only a young teenager. Her faith and obedience to God are what helped her each step of the way along the path God had for her.

Mary responded to Elizabeth by singing a song:

"My soul glorifies the Lord
and my spirit rejoices in God my Savior,
for he has been mindful
of the humble state of his servant.
From now on all generations will call me blessed,
for the Mighty One has done great things for me—
holy is his name.
His mercy extends to those who fear him,
from generation to generation.
He has performed mighty deeds with his arm;
he has scattered those who are proud in their
inmost thoughts.

He has brought down rulers from their thrones
　　but has lifted up the humble.
He has filled the hungry with good things
　　but has sent the rich away empty.
He has helped his servant Israel, remembering
　　to be merciful
to Abraham and his descendants forever,
　　just as he promised our ancestors" (Luke 1:46–55).

This was a beautiful expression of Mary's faith.

Even though she was young, her heart was filled with joy because of who God is. Another neat thing about Mary's song is that she was quoting the Psalms. It's encouraging to see a girl so young who was very much connected to the Word of God. The Bible also shows that Jesus came from the line of King David, who wrote many of the psalms that Mary referred to in her song.

David sang, "Praise the LORD, my soul; all my inmost being, praise his holy name" (Psalm 103:1). Mary sang the same, also saying that her soul brings God glory (Luke 1:46) and that

CLUES

Mary's song reminds us to always praise God, for He is worthy. God gives us grace. He fills our hearts and keeps all His promises.

God's name is holy (v. 49). And if you read Psalm 8, you will find David singing these words: "What is mankind that you are mindful of them?" (v. 4). In

Psalm 138, David again reflected on this same topic: "Though the L<small>ORD</small> is exalted, he looks kindly on the lowly" (v. 6).

Mary stayed with Elizabeth for three months and then returned home to Nazareth.

2

O Holy Night

Over two thousand years ago, when Mary was about to give birth to baby Jesus, an order was given saying that a census should be taken. A census is when the government counts the number of people living in certain areas. At this time in history, the Roman Empire was in control of all the lands that were around in the times of Jesus. The emperor was a man named Caesar Augustus. He had been in charge for twenty-five years, and plans for celebrations were under way.

The order required everyone to travel to their hometowns to register and pay taxes. Joseph was from Bethlehem, so he took Mary with him and left Nazareth.

The journey for Mary and Joseph would have

been about eighty miles total. They most likely traveled to Jerusalem first and then made their way on to Bethlehem. Mary and Joseph probably made the trek with a group of people who were also going to different towns to register for the census. The trip wasn't easy for Mary since she was several months into her pregnancy (Luke 2:4–5). Also, their route would have taken them through a land called Samaria. The Samaritans weren't friends with the Jewish people, so this would have added stress to Mary's already overwhelmed heart. The whole journey likely took them more than a week to complete, and Mary probably made the trip riding on the back of a donkey.

Joseph and Mary arrived in Bethlehem and tried to find room at an inn. Mary must have been very tired, but she soon heard that there was no

space available for them. Many people were traveling because of the census, and all the places to stay were already occupied. And because Joseph and Mary were poor, no accommodations were made for them. Can you imagine? Mary was so close to having baby Jesus, but there was nowhere for her and Joseph to go. At some point, after hearing there wasn't a room for them, Mary and Joseph were given permission to stay in a stable. This might have been a cave close to the inn where the other guests stayed.

A stable is where cattle were kept. Even though we don't know for sure what Mary was thinking, we can be certain that she was not very comfortable. Worn out from the pregnancy and the long, hard trip, Mary had to wonder where God was in all this. She knew that her baby was special and that the Holy Spirit was with her,

 **CLUES**

Everything about this holy night seemed the opposite of how Jesus, the King of all kings, should have entered the world. But Mary chose to believe God was on her side and hadn't forgotten about her and the baby.

but her emotions in the moment had to be overwhelming. Still, Mary trusted God. She knew that God was in charge and that He wouldn't let her down.

As soon as Jesus was born, Mary wrapped Jesus in cloths and put Him down to sleep in a manger. The manger was a trough, likely carved

from stone, from which the animals ate their food.

While Mary and Joseph were huddled with the dirty animals in the stable, caring for baby Jesus, another group of people were taking care of important things. Some shepherds were living out in the nearby fields watching over all their flocks, keeping them safe from wild animals and thieves. Sometime during the night, "an angel of the Lord appeared to them, and the glory of the Lord shone

around them, and they were terrified" (Luke 2:9). Just like Mary and Joseph had no idea of the great and awesome things God had in store for their lives, so too were the shepherds unaware of the beautiful and mighty life change they were about to experience.

Even though the shepherds were terrified, the angel tried to calm them and told them not to be afraid. The angel went on to explain that a Savior had been born in Bethlehem and then instructed the men to go and find baby Jesus in the manger.

The shepherds hurried and found Mary, Joseph, and the baby, just as they were told! The shepherds quickly spread the good news about what they had witnessed. Mary, on the other hand, "treasured up all these things and pondered them in her heart" (Luke 2:19). That means Mary held on to these moments and reflected on them in quiet meditation. This holy night, and everything it stood for, would remain in Mary's heart forever.

Shortly after His birth, Mary and Joseph gave their new baby the name Jesus, just as the angel had told them. Jesus. Messiah. Savior of the

World. Redeemer. How proud Mary must have
been as she watched strangers' lives change and
their hearts open when they came into contact
with her son.

Not long after
the miraculous and
beautiful birth of
Jesus, Joseph and
Mary took Him to the
temple in Jerusalem
to present Him to the
Lord. There, the Bible
says, they met a man
named Simeon who
was very nice. Simeon saw baby Jesus and held
Him in his arms. He called out to God, saying that
his eyes had seen the Savior!

Mary and Joseph marveled at what was said
about Jesus (Luke 2:33). A prophet named Anna,

 **CLUES**

God takes care of His people.
He knows there will come
times in our lives when we
will not understand and
may even feel overwhelmed.
But just like with Mary and
Joseph, and even the shepherds, God will also come to
us with reminders that we
shouldn't be afraid, because
He is with us. Always.

who was very old, stayed in the temple worshipping God day and night. She too came up to Mary and Joseph, gave thanks, and spoke highly of Jesus and talked about how He would be the One who would redeem people.

After all the jobs in Jerusalem were complete, Mary and Joseph returned to Nazareth. Jesus "grew and became strong; he was filled with wisdom, and the grace of God was on him" (Luke 2:40).

Wise Men Visit

The birth of Jesus was very special. Soon people everywhere were hearing the news of His arrival. While Mary was raising her newborn son, wise men (magi) from the East came to Jerusalem and asked where they could find the "king of the Jews" (Matthew 2:2). When they arrived, the men approached a king named Herod, who wasn't a good man. The king told them to report back after they found Jesus. He said it was because he also wanted to go and worship Jesus; but truthfully, Herod had different plans. He didn't want Jesus taking over his role as king, so he made an evil plan to end Jesus' life.

The magi left Herod and went on their way. Soon they found the house they were looking for.

They found Mary and Jesus at home. Even though we aren't given specifics in the Bible, we can imagine the look on Mary's face when these strangers appeared at her door saying that they had followed a star in the night sky to find them.

The magi explained the reason for their visit. And like the shepherds before them, the men bowed down and worshipped Jesus. Their worship of Jesus gives more proof that He was the King of kings they had been looking for. Mary watched in awe as the men presented Jesus with gifts of gold, frankincense, and myrrh (Matthew 2:11). These gifts would help Mary and Joseph avoid staying in poverty. God had blessed the young couple and their young son.

Sometime during this visit, the wise men were warned in a dream not to return to King Herod. They said goodbye to Mary, Joseph, and Jesus and took a different route back to their homes.

After the men left, an angel came to Joseph in a dream and told him to take Jesus and Mary and escape to Egypt. The angel told Joseph about King Herod's wicked plans to hurt Jesus. So, under cover of night, Joseph took Mary and Jesus and left

Bethlehem. They headed for the faraway land of Egypt where they stayed until Herod died.

Instead of returning to Bethlehem, Mary and Joseph traveled to Nazareth. They made this decision because Herod's son Archelaus reigned over Bethlehem, and they didn't want to risk any harm coming to Jesus.

All the traveling and all the escapes. Visits from angels, shepherds, and wise men. Mary

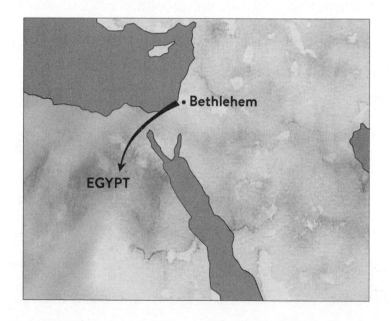

couldn't have imagined a more bizarre story, but she remained faithful to God through it all. She knew that God could have changed the way things happened to her and her family. Jesus could have come into the world in a totally different, much more triumphant, way. Definitely not in an animal pen on a cold, dark night with nothing but strips of cloth to keep Him warm. That's not how the King of kings should enter the scene, right?

But that's exactly how God wanted it to be. And Mary's heart embraced the plans and desires of

 CLUES

The Bible doesn't tell us how long Mary, Joseph, and Jesus stayed in Egypt. Some say anywhere between months and years. But whatever the length of time, it's important to focus on Mary's obedience to God's will. God could have made a way for Herod to be taken off the throne, but instead God chose to have Mary and Joseph take Jesus far away from their home.

her heavenly Father. She didn't argue or complain. Mary just trusted God's will and humbled herself to accept the strange circumstances that surrounded the birth of Jesus.

4

Jesus at the Temple

When time came for the Passover festival, Mary and Joseph took Jesus to Jerusalem for this annual event. Passover was a time when the people celebrated and remembered how God freed their ancestors from slavery in Egypt. You might remember a man named Moses. He was the man who helped free the Israelites from under the pharaoh's rule. During that time, God sent ten plagues over Egypt. During the last plague, the Spirit of the Lord passed over the homes of the Israelites, keeping them from harm.

Mary and Joseph followed the rules and obeyed the laws. They were dedicated Jews living according to the law of Moses. In those days, a boy of twelve was considered to be completing his last year of preparation for religious life. Up to that point in a young man's life, the parents (especially the father) would teach the boy the commandments. At the end of the twelfth year, a formal ceremony took place in which the son would become a *bar mitzvah,* or "son of the commandment."

Jesus was around twelve years old at the time and was strong and filled with wisdom, and the grace of God was on Him (Luke 2:40). It seems as though Jesus had chosen this crucial time to show everyone that He had a unique relationship with God and an extraordinary understanding of God's law.

When the Passover festival was over, Mary and Joseph headed back home to Nazareth. When they left, Jesus stayed behind in Jerusalem. His parents were unaware that Jesus wasn't traveling with them. Remember, they were most likely traveling with a large group of family and friends and had assumed Jesus was in the crowd. Mary traveled for a full day before she began looking for Jesus among her relatives and friends.

After searching for a long time, Mary could not find her son, so both she and Joseph returned to Jerusalem to look for Jesus. Surely they worried

about where He was or what might have happened to Him.

After three whole days of searching, Mary found Jesus in the temple courts, "sitting among the teachers, listening to them and asking them

CLUES

Jesus traveling apart from His parents suggests that they trusted Him. He was trustworthy enough that Mary didn't worry. A good lesson here is to act respectfully to your parents and teachers. Let your actions show others that you care more about doing God's will than your own.

questions" (Luke 2:46). Mary stood there astonished, not only at the fact that she had found her son but by the looks on the people's faces who were listening to Jesus speak. "Everyone who heard him was amazed at his understanding and his answers" (Luke 2:47).

Mary, however, was not all pleased with Jesus. She said, "Son, why have you treated us like this? Your father and I have been anxiously searching for you" (Luke 2:48).

Jesus had an answer ready for His mother. He asked her why they were

CLUES

Mary and Joseph's three-day ordeal of searching and painfully regretting losing track of their son foreshadowed the pain that would come when Mary had to endure the crucifixion and burial of Jesus. After another three days of agony and grieving her son's death, a day of rejoicing would come when Mary realized that Jesus had conquered death!

searching for Him. He said, "Didn't you know I had to be in my Father's house?" (Luke 2:49). The Bible says that Mary and Joseph didn't understand what Jesus meant by His question. It's clear, however, that Jesus understood that His heavenly Father had sent Him on a mission to become the Savior of the world. Also, Jesus knew that His relationship to God was more important than any other relationship.

Jesus was basically telling His parents that He had come into this world to do His Father's business. After the meeting back at the temple, Jesus did follow Mary and Joseph home to Nazareth and "was obedient to them" (Luke 2:51). The next verse in Luke's account is an important one as we learn about Mary's personality and what made her special. It says that she "treasured all these things in her heart" (2:51). What things? The words Jesus was saying. Even though she might not have understood everything Jesus was doing, Mary chose to keep all of it in her heart, believing that as time went on things would be made clear to her.

Mary watched her son grow wiser and stronger. She watched as He gained favor with both God and man.

5

A Special Wedding

In a remote village away from the hustle of Jerusalem, a couple was getting married in a place called Cana in Galilee. Mary, Jesus, and His disciples were at the wedding celebration. The Bible doesn't mention Joseph, because he had most likely passed away by this time in Mary's life. The wedding was a big celebration, and everyone was having a good time.

At some point, after the people had been eating and drinking, the Bible says that Mary went up to Jesus and told Him that the hosts of the party had run out of wine. Jesus answered, "Woman, why do you involve me? . . . My hour has not yet come" (John 2:4). He was explaining to Mary that there is an appointed time for everything in God's plan.

Jesus was saying that He answers only to God.

And the "hour" referred to the hour when Jesus

would die for the sins of the world. Jesus con-

firmed that He would be obedient to God above

all others. He was setting the example that even though she was His mother, Mary would not be treated differently than any of God's other children.

Jesus did perform a miracle to help Mary and the wedding guests. He probably also performed it to give the guests a picture of His upcoming sacrifice on the cross. And even though Jesus rebuked Mary (told her seriously that He had come to do God's will), she was confident in her relationship and worth in Jesus. She went on to tell the servants, "Do whatever he tells you" (John 2:5).

Mary stood by and watched Jesus tell the servants to fill six stone jars (each held twenty to thirty gallons). The attendants obeyed and filled the ceremonial jars to the brim. These were not jars used for drinking. These jars would be used for the ritual washing for purification. This means the people would have religious ceremonies and use the jars of water to represent the washing away of bad choices.

Next, Jesus told them to draw out some water and take it to the man who was in charge of the banquet. When the master tasted the water, he was amazed because it was actually wine. Another interesting note is that the

 **CLUES**

Mary set an example for all of us as she showed us bold-ness in approaching Jesus as the answer to and pro-vider for all our problems. And even though this was the first public miracle that Jesus performed, Mary knew that her son was ca-pable of great things. Mary set a good example for us not only to ask God for help for ourselves but also to ask Him to help others in need. We bring God glory when we lift others up in prayer. She knew there were other ways to solve the problem, but going to Jesus is always the best answer.

bridegroom was in charge of the wine and would have been responsible for seeing that it did not run out before the party was over.

The Bible says that Jesus decided to perform the miracle to display His glory. Also, because of this miracle, the disciples believed in Him. Jesus showed the wedding guests—and us today—that He alone can provide what man cannot. Mary knew that all this grace shown at the wedding in Cana had nothing to do with her.

After the wedding feast, Mary traveled with Jesus and His brothers and disciples to Capernaum where they stayed a few days. Surely their conversation along the way was about the miracle Jesus had performed at the wedding!

6

A Misunderstanding, the Cross, and Everything After

Time passed after the wedding feast. Jesus entered a house with His friends and planned to eat a meal there. As usual, a large crowd gathered inside. People had heard about Jesus and all His love and healing power. They poured into the house to try and get Jesus to help them too. The gathering was so big that Jesus and His followers were not able to eat.

His family heard about this and came to get Jesus. They came to take Him away, thinking that He was out of His mind. They thought He might be tired because of all the work He had been doing.

The teachers of the law came down from Jerusalem and said that Jesus was possessed by the devil because He was driving out demons. They didn't believe Jesus was who He said He was, so these men were looking for a way to get rid of Jesus.

Jesus firmly corrected them, saying they

should not blaspheme (or make fun of) the Holy Spirit. He was trying to tell the people that He was doing God's work and that indeed He had not lost His mind.

When Mary arrived with Jesus' brothers, they stood outside the house where Jesus was. They sent someone in to call Jesus out. The crowd inside told Jesus that Mary and His brothers were looking for Him. Jesus answered with a question: "Who are my mother and my brothers?" (Mark 3:33). Without waiting for an answer, Jesus told those gathered around Him that whoever does God's will is His family.

***

The next time Mary is mentioned by name in the Bible is when Jesus was being crucified. This was the darkest hour. Mary had to endure great pain and sadness as the soldiers made Jesus carry His cross all through the streets of Jerusalem and then out of the city to a place called Golgotha ("the place of the skull"). Mary watched as the soldiers nailed Jesus to the cross. She saw the sign that was placed over His head: THIS IS JESUS, THE KING OF THE JEWS. The soldiers wrote the sign in Latin, Greek, and Aramaic to make sure everyone around could read the charge made against Jesus.

Mary, who had been storing the memories of Jesus in her heart, now understood how true that sign on her son's cross really was. The Bible tells us the chief priests complained. They wanted the sign to read that Jesus "claimed to be king of the Jews" (John 19:21). The sign remained, and the soldiers divided up the Lord's clothes.

Poor Mary had a place right at the foot of the cross. She was there with her sister and Mary Magdalene. Also, the disciple John was there. Jesus spoke to both of them from the cross. " 'Woman, here is your son, and to the disciple, Here is your mother.' " (John 19:26–27). From that day, John took Mary into his home to live.

As the sadness continued, Mary watched as Jesus took His last breath. And after His body was taken down off the cross, another friend of Jesus',

a man named Joseph of Arimathea, came and took His body away to be buried in a new tomb nearby. The Bible doesn't tell us what Mary was doing at that point, but she was likely overcome with grief and emotion. However, she would have been fa-

miliar with her son's teachings and His words that spoke of rising from the grave after three days. Somewhere in Mary's heart, hope was waiting and looking forward to a day when all her tears would be wiped away.

***

The last time Mary is mentioned by name in the Bible happens after Jesus rose from the grave. Jesus appeared to His apostles for a period of forty days, teaching them more truths about the kingdom of God. One day, Jesus gave them a command not to leave the city of Jerusalem until they received the gift of the Holy Spirit. Jesus told them that with the Holy Spirit, they would be His witnesses to the ends of the earth. Just after saying this, Jesus was taken up into heaven and a cloud hid Him from them.

The apostles stood staring at the sky when two men dressed in white clothing asked what they were looking at. The two men went on to explain that Jesus would return in the same way He went to heaven.

All of Jesus' friends, including Mary and His

brothers, gathered together, constantly praying to God. They were celebrating because Jesus was alive. They were also looking for direction. After all, they had just watched Jesus go up into heaven and were left to wonder about their future.

Now that we've investigated the story of Mary, mother of Jesus, it's time to study some lessons that we can learn from her life. We will look at ten "Power-Ups" that will help us connect scripture to our daily lives. Memory verses will go along with each Power-Up to help us plant God's truth in our hearts.

Power-Up #1:

LET YOUR LIFE GLORIFY GOD.

Mary prayed for her soul to make God magnified. You know when you look at something through a magnifying glass, it gets bigger. When people look at your life, do they see a bigger picture of who God is? This is what Mary wanted for her life. She was focused on letting her actions point people to God in big ways. When we read our Bibles and plant God's words deep in our hearts, we will live a life that brings Him glory.

It's one thing to read a few Bible stories and listen to sermons in church, but it's another thing to live out your beliefs. Mary was so familiar with the Old Testament that she was able to sing out her song of praise as she quoted scripture. Think about your schedule and come up with a plan to have a daily quiet time with God. This will help you know God more and understand how to live a life that makes much of Him. This is a good goal to make as we work on powering up our daily walks with Jesus.

Think of ways you can make more of God. Ask Him for strength and opportunities to turn people toward His mercy and grace. Let God use you like He used Mary, by sacrificing your time and resources to share the good news of Jesus. Do things that let other people know they are loved by God. Memorize scripture so you can plant the Word of God in your heart so you will be able to recite verses of praise and instruction as you follow God's will for your life.

MEMORY VERSE. "My soul glorifies the Lord." LUKE 1:46

Power-Up #2:

REJOICE THAT GOD IS YOUR SAVIOR.

The next part of Mary's song gives us another goal to strive for in living life for God. She knew that her spirit was the fullest when it was praising her Savior. When we find our greatest joy in Jesus, we will be completely satisfied. The enemy will try to tempt God's children into finding their happiness in other people and material possessions. You may find yourself wishing you had more than what you have. You may find yourself complaining because things didn't go exactly the way you wanted them to.

But God wants us to rely on Him in all situations. Whether your day is going great or your heart is filled with sadness, God wants you to know how much you mean to Him. Try to praise Him daily and let Him carry you in His mighty arms. This helps take your eyes off yourself and put them on God. Having a grateful heart keeps your priorities straight. You will get to a place where praising God becomes a habit. Instead of complaining about what didn't go right, you will find yourself contemplating all the wonderful things God is and thanking Him for loving you.

Be happy with where God has you. Thank Him for providing for all your needs. Trust that He has the best plans for you. Trust that He wants everything you want and more. Spend your time finding ways to praise Him. Rejoice that God has saved you from the chains of sin. You will make mistakes, but the difference is that you're forgiven. Like Mary, we need to let our lives announce the joy that we find only in Jesus.

MEMORY VERSE: "My spirit rejoices in God my Savior." LUKE 1:47

Power-Up #3:
GOD KNOWS YOU.

What a strong, encouraging truth to take with you in your days, to know that God knows your name! The Creator of the universe knows you and thinks about you. He considers all the wonderful plans He has for your life and leads you daily to all the things He has in store for you. Mary said that God was *mindful* of her (Luke 1:48). This means that God cared about every detail of her life, and since God doesn't change, we can be confident that He does the same for us today.

You are the only *you* God made! There never has been another *you,* and there never will be another. As you think about this powerful truth, let it move your heart as you begin to ponder how much kingdom work you can accomplish for God's glory. What special talents has God given you? What are you really good at doing? How can you take those gifts and use them to bless others and point people to Jesus as their Savior? God thinks about you all day long. He celebrates your accomplishments, and He understands your sadness. You are not alone. God is always thinking about you.

God made you special. He thought long and hard about how to make you unique. He made no mistakes when He created you. Don't forget that truth! He knows all of you, and the Bible promises that He has great plans for your life. You aren't like one of those wind-up toys, as if God sets you in motion and then leaves you on your own to go on random paths. You are an original masterpiece whom God carries through all the hours and days He has planned for you. Celebrate your wonderful Creator today. He really does care!

MEMORY VERSE: "He has been mindful of the humble state of his servant." LUKE 1:48

Power-Up #4:
GOD BLESSES YOU.

When Mary prayed, she said that generations of people would call her blessed. She wasn't being prideful. She was simply confident in her identity in Jesus. She knew her worth wasn't found in worldly things. As a believer, your life, identity, and worth are all wrapped up in Jesus. Our lesson here to power up our daily living is to remember that we are leaving a legacy of mercy and grace. People are always watching us. They may never tell us, but they are looking at how we treat each other and how we talk. They are seeing if our words match our actions.

We should live a life that makes people want to praise God's name forever. Our choices should reflect the light of Jesus in a dark world. Think about all the ways God has blessed you. Let this fill your heart with gladness as you go through your day. Be confident that God loves you and is always at work in your life. Be certain that He calls you to step out in faith to do big things. This begins the work of creating a legacy where future family members will share stories about your wonderful kingdom work!

God knows what we need before we even ask Him for anything. He gives us what we need and so much more. When you realize just how much He blesses you, things start to look different. You begin to nurture a heart of greater thankfulness and compassion. Being aware of your blessings helps you to share those blessings with others. Maybe you could start a prayer journal and list all the ways God is blessing you. That could drive your prayers and praises throughout the year. It will also help you see how God is working and moving in your life.

MEMORY VERSE: "From now on all generations will call me blessed." LUKE 1:48

Power-Up #5:

GOD DOES GREAT THINGS FOR YOU.

God is always doing great things for us. Since God doesn't change, we need to always remember that He wants what's best for us. He doesn't walk away or stop listening. Live each day knowing that God is your Mighty One. He is the source of all your hope. God will never walk away from you or change the way He feels about your heart. Pray and wait. Know that God doesn't make mistakes. God is working in your life in mighty ways to bless you.

Live by the strength that comes from the same One who put the stars in the sky and carved out the massive oceans and filled them with water. God knows what you need because He made you! Whatever you're facing, God will do great things for you because He loves you more than anything. Trust this even when the day is long and you feel tired. Trust that God is doing great things for you even when happiness seems just out of reach.

Wrap your mind around the fact that God is *for* you. He wants to see you thrive and be a powerful witness to His kingdom. He wants you to know that you aren't just another person lost in the crowd. God is cheering you on to lead the crowd for Jesus! It's exciting to think about all the possibilities you have in front of you. Your life will continue to shine by God's radiant light and continually remind the world that His name is forever holy.

MEMORY VERSE: "The Mighty One has done great things for me—holy is his name." LUKE 1:49

Power-Up #6:

GOD GIVES YOU HIS MERCY.

God knows what you're going through. He sees the path you're on and walks beside you. Just like He did for Mary, God will also show you mercy all the time. When Mary was nervous about the news of being pregnant, God showed mercy and sent an angel to help soothe her. When Mary needed reassurance, God brought her to Elizabeth and let them connect with the Holy Spirit. When Jesus was older and they were at the wedding feast, Mary found comfort in the power of her son's ability to provide.

God is there for you today. He is ready to give you mercy and lift you up because He cares about you so much. Know that His mercy is active. It picks you up from the pit of your mistakes and bad choices and sets you down on the solid ground of God's truth. His mercy holds your hand and reassures you that everything will be okay. He thinks you're awesome, and His mercy reminds you of that truth. God wants you to know that He listens to you and thinks about you. Be encouraged by how much you mean to Him, and live today for His kingdom!

God's mercy showers you with second chances. His mercy means that when you mess up or make a bad choice, God is not going to walk away from you. Ever. From the very beginning of the Bible, God didn't leave Adam and Eve alone in the garden. He went after them and provided a sacrifice and clothing. God solved their sin problem. God's mercy solves your problems too. You have to work hard and honor Him in everything you do, but when things don't go the way you hoped, God's mercy reminds you that He is in control and He cares for you.

MEMORY VERSE: "His mercy extends to those who fear him." LUKE 1:50

Power-Up #7:

GOD IS MIGHTY AND CARRIES YOUR BURDENS.

The One who made you and loves you is also strong enough to carry you. Whatever you're going through, God is bigger! Even though we can't imagine how sad Mary must have been to see Jesus carry His cross to Calvary, it must have been amazing to see her face when she realized that Jesus defeated the grave and rose again! Mary understood pain and loss. She saw how the cross weighed heavy on her son's back. She experienced loss when, as a youth, Jesus had stayed behind in the temple after she and Joseph had left for home.

No power on earth is stronger than God. Put your trust in Him, and He will never let you down. Just as Mary relied on God to get her through the hard times, we need to do the same. God loves you and is there to carry you through it all. No matter how alone you might feel, God is always with you.

He holds you and never lets go. This should reassure you that nothing gets to you before it goes through God. He is your shield and protector. Give Him your hardships. Give Him your sadness. God is there to give you rest.

God is the Rock on which your life is built. No storm or trial is bigger than God. Nothing in this world is strong enough to pull you down and away from Him. He protects you with His mighty arms. He wipes away tears and encourages you because He is full of love and compassion. Remember that He is for you in all things, and His love is forever.

MEMORY VERSE: "He has performed mighty deeds with his arm." LUKE 1:51

Power-Up #8:

GOD LIFTS UP THE HUMBLE.

Mary obeyed God and lived a humble life. She knew that God had a plan for her, and she was satisfied with that plan. Mary wanted God to be in charge of her life. It's easy to get wrapped up in wanting more than you have or even wishing you had all the things your friends have. But God has a plan for you, and He will give you everything you need to be successful. He doesn't want you distracted by running after stuff.

Being humble means relying on God all the time, not just when we need something. Let Him show you the paths He wants you to take, and be content with them. Being humble means accepting that God's plans may not be what we want but still being okay because we know that God wants what's best for His children. Being humble often means putting others' needs before your own. It's not easy, but that is the example Jesus set for us, and He guarantees to lift up and help those who live out of humility rather than selfish pride.

At times you will feel like being selfish. This is when you have an opportunity to pray and ask God for help in being humble to put other people first. Putting other people's needs before your own helps you to become more like Jesus!

MEMORY VERSE: "[He] has lifted up the humble." LUKE 1:52

Power-Up #9:

GOD MEETS ALL YOUR NEEDS.

Mary knew God was her provider. She understood that He was the One who gave her everything she needed. She knew that He had chosen her to give birth to baby Jesus and gave her all the many blessings that came with being His mother. Mary understood that everything she had came from God and not from her hard work. God was in control of her life, and He provided for her and her family.

God does the same thing for us. He meets us where we are, no matter what situation we find ourselves in, and takes care of our needs. Even if we're having a bad day and God seems far away, the truth will always be that He is with us. Be confident that you are very special to Him. The Bible is full of examples of how much God provides. When people were hungry, God gave them bread from heaven. When they were outnumbered in battle, God gave them protection. And when people needed a Savior, God gave them Jesus! He knows what we need! Talk to God. Tell Him what you need. He knows and loves you. Be amazed at how He will bless your life!

This doesn't mean that God is a vending machine who will give you whatever you ask for. It means that God knows the best things for you. He decides. Knowing this will free you from worrying about things. Give everything to God and be free to follow Him.

MEMORY VERSE: "He has filled the hungry with good things." LUKE 1:53

Power-Up #10:

GOD IS HELPFUL.

Remember how Mary lived a humble life, connected to Jesus all the time? She knew that He was the source of her hope and provider for all that mattered. Mary relied on Jesus to be her helper, and that's a great way for us to live today. Like Mary, we need to get in the habit of turning to Jesus.

From that humble start in the stable, holding baby Jesus began the unbreakable bond of mother and child. In that moment, as Mary held Jesus, she knew that her baby would grow and become so much more than her son. Jesus would become her source for living.

In the beginning of His ministry, at the wedding feast, Mary didn't hesitate to ask Jesus to turn the water into wine. Jesus took care of His mother then, and because of His great love for her, He took care of her at the end of His earthly life. From the cross, Jesus made sure His friend John would take care of Mary.

Turning to Jesus and relying on Him will help us become the people we were made to be, and in turn, God will be glorified.

MEMORY VERSE: "He has helped his servant." LUKE 1:54

Kingdom Files:

Who Is Jesus?

Dear Reading Detective,

Welcome to Kingdom Files! You're now a very important part of the Kingdom Files investigation—a series of really cool biographies all found in the Bible. Each case you investigate focuses on an important Bible character and is separated into three sections to make your time fun and interesting. First, you'll find the **Fact File**, which contains key information about a specific Bible character whom God called to do big things for His kingdom. Next, you'll read through an **Action File** that lays out Bible events showing the character in action. And finally, the **Power File** is where you'll find valuable information and memory verses to help you see how God is working in your life too. Along the way, **Clue Boxes** will offer applications to help you keep track of your thoughts as you make your way through the files. You can also use these sections to record questions you might have along Jesus' journey. Write down any questions, and then ask your parents to get them involved in your quest.

Before you begin, know this: not only did God have plans for the Bible characters you'll read about in the Kingdom Files, but Jeremiah 29:11 says that God has big plans for you too! I pray that *Kingdom Files: Who Is Jesus?* helps you get a bigger picture of God and that you will see just how much He loves you!

Blessings,
M.K.

Name: **JESUS**

Occupation: **Savior of the world**

From: **heaven**

Years Active: **forever**

Kingdom Work: **left His heavenly throne and humbled Himself to become a man; preached the Good News of God; died on a cross for the forgiveness of sins; and rose on the third day and conquered death!**

Mini Timeline of Earthly Ministry:

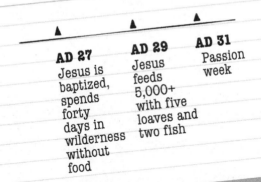

AD 27
Jesus is baptized, spends forty days in wilderness without food

AD 29
Jesus feeds 5,000+ with five loaves and two fish

AD 31
Passion week

Key Stats:
+ Son of God
+ Savior of the world
+ Our Good Shepherd

1

Early Life!

Jesus was born in a town called Bethlehem, located in Israel. Bethlehem means "House of Bread," which is interesting because Jesus is called the Bread of Life. Out of all the people in the Kingdom Files series, Jesus is the most important for so many reasons.

Jesus was born to His earthly parents, Mary and Joseph. An angel came to Mary and said that she would miraculously have a baby and that she should name Him Jesus.

When it was time for Mary to give birth, she and Joseph could not find a proper place to stay, so they had to make do in stable—a place where animals are kept. And so Jesus was born in a manger alongside the animals. The Savior of the world was born in a dusty, dirty place.

A very sad thing happened after Jesus was born. There was

CLUES

In the Old Testament book of Micah, the prophet declared that Bethlehem would be where the Messiah would be born (5:2)!

a very evil king by the name of Herod the Great who was put in charge by the Romans. He was supposed to govern the Jewish people who lived in Israel. You might be familiar with the fact that when Jesus was born, a bright star appeared in the sky. Three wise men from the

East began following the star to find Jesus because they wanted to meet Him. On their journey, they met King Herod and told him the reason for their travels. Herod did not want to give up his power, so he ordered that every baby in Bethlehem should be killed. This sounds like an insane reaction. It was, but Herod was afraid.

The idea that this baby Jesus could become a king was a threat to Herod's reign. He loved telling everyone what to do, and he surely didn't want to give up all his power. Fear pushed him to make a terrible decision.

But God is a mighty protector, and He sent an angel to warn Joseph of Herod's evil plan. Joseph obeyed and took Mary and baby Jesus to Egypt until they received news that King Herod had died. When the time was right, Joseph led his wife and Jesus back to Israel. But instead of going to Bethlehem, they went to a town called Nazareth.

The Bible tells us that when Jesus was twelve, His family traveled to Jerusalem to celebrate the annual Passover festival. Jesus became separated from His parents—He went into the temple and had deep conversations about God. The people were amazed at how such a young man could know as much as Jesus knew. Eventually Mary found Jesus, who said, "Didn't you know I had to be in my Father's house?" (Luke 2:49).

There's not much written about what Jesus did from the time He was twelve until the time He began His earthly ministry. We do know that Joseph was called a "builder," and that the custom of the day was for a father to train his son in his occupation. Most people say Joseph was a carpenter, and that very well may have been the case. However, many scholars believe that a more accurate job description would be stonemason because trees were, and still are, scarce in the region Jesus grew up in and the majority of homes are built out of rock.

A stonemason is a person who creates buildings out of stone. This person knows how to take a rough stone found in nature and craft it into a shape that is ready to use for making structures. The mason would typically use a mallet (a type of hammer) and chisel (a type of blade) to cut the stone.

Either way, Jesus worked very hard and helped His father every day.

The next information the Bible shares about the life of Jesus was when He was thirty years old. He left His hometown and went to the wilderness by the Jordan River to be baptized by John the Baptist (Mark 1:9). After that, Jesus went into the desert for forty days. Jesus fasted during this time, which meant He didn't have anything to eat. You can imagine how hungry Jesus was. Fasting helped Him focus on God because it was making Him rely on His Father for strength.

This is also the time when the devil tried to tempt Jesus. The first temptation dealt with turning stones into bread. Remember, because Jesus was so hungry it makes sense that the enemy tried to attack Him with this food temptation. But Jesus was ready for the attack! He replied to the devil's taunt by quoting Deuteronomy 8:3 that says man doesn't live just on bread, but on "every word that comes from the mouth of the LORD."

The enemy tries to trick people into thinking that true happiness and fulfillment come from all the things that they can do. Jesus turned this thinking upside down when He said that everything that counts comes only from God. The devil took Jesus to the top of the temple in the city and said that Jesus should jump off because the angels would save Him. Jesus replied that people shouldn't test God. Finally, the devil took Jesus to the top of a nearby

mountain. From there they could see "all the kingdoms of the world and their splendor" (Matthew 4:8). The devil said he would give it all to Jesus if He would only worship him. Jesus stood His ground and reminded the enemy that God is the only One to be worshipped and served.

After a long time in the desert, Jesus went to Galilee and began calling people to follow Him and become His disciples. Jesus told His friends that His mission was to seek out the lost and help people know and understand that they are loved.

Teaching and Parables

Jesus started His ministry by teaching in the synagogues and telling people about God and healing people of their diseases.

Early on, large crowds began to gather, and Jesus went up a mountainside. His disciples went with Him, but the crowds followed too. That day Jesus taught a handful of lessons called the Beatitudes.

The first lesson Jesus taught was, "Blessed are the poor in spirit, for theirs is the kingdom of heaven"

CLUES

Beatitudes comes from the Latin word for happiness. In them, Jesus taught simple but powerful lessons.

(Matthew 5:3). Jesus told His followers that they should work hard to avoid being selfish.

The next lesson Jesus gave was on being sorry when people do things that are against God's will for us. He said, "Blessed are those who mourn, for they will be comforted" (Matthew 5:4).

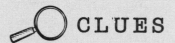

CLUES

When we get rid of the idea of having everything go our way, then our hearts will be open to hear what God has to teach us.

Another point Jesus wanted His followers to understand was the importance of having a right attitude. He said, "Blessed are the meek, for they will inherit the earth" (Matthew 5:5).

Jesus continued His teaching by saying, "Blessed are those who hunger and thirst for

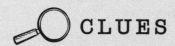

CLUES

When we sin, we are saying no to all the good things Jesus has for us. In this lesson, Jesus is telling us that we will find blessing when we are sorry for our mistakes and ask God to forgive us.

righteousness, for they will be filled" (Matthew 5:6). This means that God wants us to crave Him and His blessings for our lives. Jesus wants us to remember that when we stay connected to Him, our hearts remain full. If we desire other stuff like popularity or material things, then we will always want

CLUES

Meek doesn't mean "weak." This is important to remember because Jesus was saying that meek is an attitude of respect and humility. Someone who is meek isn't selfish. They want the good things that God has for them. People who are meek are kind to others and demonstrate patience. A meek person doesn't become angry at others but instead offers forgiveness because they know that Jesus forgave them.

more. Jesus also wants to make sure we care for others who may need our help.

"Blessed are the merciful, for they will be shown mercy," Jesus told the crowd (Matthew

5:7). When we are merciful, we show compassion to others. Showing mercy means caring about and forgiving our friends. It means being kind and showing sympathy to let other people know that they matter.

Jesus also said, "Blessed are the pure in heart, for they will see God" (Matthew 5:8).

"Blessed are the peacemakers, for they will be

CLUES

Right living is what Jesus wants from His followers. Reading your Bible and praying for God's strength are ways we can keep our hearts connected to Jesus.

called children of God" (Matthew 5:9). Jesus shared His peace everywhere He went. Being a blessing to others wherever you are is a good way to bring peace. Make it a habit to help others know that they can find rest in Jesus. Make a habit of leaving people feeling the peaceful joy that comes from a relationship with Jesus.

Jesus continued teaching, telling the crowd that there would be hard days in life. "Blessed are those who are persecuted because of righteousness, for theirs is the kingdom of heaven" (Matthew 5:10). "Blessed are you when people insult you. . .because of me. Rejoice and be glad, because great is your reward in heaven" (Matthew 5:11).

Jesus went on to say that His followers are the salt of the earth; they add meaning and give hope to a hopeless world. Jesus also added that His followers were the light of the world and that when they shine in public, God gets the glory. He made a big deal about the importance of not worrying. Jesus told

 CLUES

Jesus is saying that when you stick up for your faith, some people may not like it. There might even come a time when you get made fun of because of your faith. Jesus says not to worry because He is always with you. He will guard your heart and mind.

the people that life was so much more than food and clothes. He reminded them that God knows exactly what they need and would provide for His children every time (Matthew 6:33).

Another way Jesus taught people was through the use of parables. These stories were made up

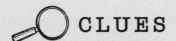 CLUES

All these lessons are very good for us, but we need to remember that we cannot do anything without the help of Jesus. We should pray and ask Him for the courage and power to live like He has taught. You will be able to do great things for Jesus when He is your Rock.

but helped Jesus get people to connect their hearts to things of heaven. The themes of the parables in the Bible focus on love and forgiveness, losing precious things and finding them again, the kingdom of heaven, prayer, and the end times when Jesus returns.

Jesus told the parable of the lost sheep (Matthew

18:12–14 and Luke 15:3–7). He described how a shepherd left his flock of ninety-nine sheep to go rescue one that was lost. The religious leaders, who knew Jesus, accused Him of eating with sinners. Here Jesus was teaching that He is the Good Shepherd who goes in search of people who have strayed. The parable ends with Jesus saying that there is more rejoicing in heaven over one sinner who repents than over all those who are righteous.

The next parable Jesus told is the parable of the lost coin. This story is found in Luke 15:8–10 and is about a woman who looks everywhere for a coin she had lost. The coin was worth more than a coin we think of today. The coin she had lost was called a drachma and was worth about a day's wages. The woman looked diligently for the missing coin until it was found. The coin in this parable represents a lost sinner.

A third parable Jesus told that represents a lost sinner being found is known as the parable of the prodigal son (Luke 15:11–32). A father had two sons, and the younger son asked for his share of the inheritance and moved out. After he spent all his money, the younger son was forced to work with pigs. He was so poor that the pig food actually looked pretty tasty. At that point, he realized that he needed to go back home to his family.

The father wasn't mad when the son returned but instead threw a party in celebration. The older brother was angry because he didn't think it was fair, but the father said that the point was that his younger son had been lost and now was found.

Jesus also told a few stories about the power of prayer. One of these stories is about a friend at night (Luke 11:5–8), and Jesus used this parable to remind His followers to pray and never give up. In the story, a neighbor went to another friend's house in the middle of the night and asked for bread. He said the bread was for another friend who had arrived after being on a journey. At first, the neighbor said he didn't want to be bothered, but after a while he took care of the request.

Jesus shared another parable with the same theme—the unjust judge. The story is found in Luke 18:1–8. A poor widow approached a judge to ask for help. He said no at first but then gave her what she asked for because she was so persistent.

Finally, on the same theme of prayer, Jesus told a parable about a Pharisee and a tax collector (Luke 18:9–14). Jesus used this story to teach us that when we pray we need to have a humble heart. The self-confident Pharisee thought that because he kept so many religious rituals (more than was required) he didn't need to ask God for anything. Contrast this with the tax collector who realized he was a sinner and humbly asked God for forgiveness. God showed the tax collector mercy and extended forgiveness.

In other parables, Jesus taught about the power of love and forgiveness. A popular one is called the good Samaritan, found in the gospel of Luke 10:25–37. The story is about a Jewish man who was traveling and was attacked and left hurting on the side of the road. Two people walked by and saw the man, but both refused to help him. Finally, a Samaritan came by and stopped to help the injured man. At the time Jesus told this story, Samaritans and Jews were groups of people who didn't like each other.

Another similar story is the parable of the two

debtors (Luke 7:36–50). There were two people who owed money. One owed five hundred denarii and the other fifty denarii. The lender forgave both debts. Jesus was making a point that the one who was forgiven the larger debt would be more grateful.

The last parable that Jesus told on love and forgiveness is about an unforgiving servant (Matthew 18:21–35). There were two servants who owed debts. The first servant was forgiven, but when he was asked to forgive one of his own servants, he refused. When the man in charge of the first servant found out about the man's behavior, he became angry and had the man punished.

Jesus told many other parables that taught His friends important life lessons. One was the parable of the mustard seed (Mark 4:30–32). The mustard seed is tiny but grows into a very tall plant. Jesus explained how the gospel message and the kingdom of God on earth had a very small beginning (remember Jesus was born in a manger!) but had grown very large.

Another parable is about the wise and foolish builders (found in Matthew 7:24–27). In the parable, there were two men. The wise man built his house on rock, and the foolish man built his house on sand. The rains came, and the winds were strong. The house on the rock was safe in the storm while the house built on sand fell down.

The wise man built his life on God's principles and put them into practice. And that is the only sure foundation for our lives.

Miracles

One of the many extraordinary things about Jesus is that He performed miracles. Jesus loves you, and He loved His family and friends on earth. During Jesus' earthly ministry, people He met would often ask Him for help. Some were sick. Some needed spiritual healing. Others just needed to know truth. Jesus did miracles to show that He was in charge of everything and that everything was under His supernatural command.

Early in His life, before Jesus began His public ministry, He attended a wedding with His mother and some of His friends. The celebration was in a town called Cana, which is near Nazareth. This was where Jesus performed His first miracle of changing water into wine. (You can find this story in your Bible in John 2:1–11.) During the party, the servants were worried because the wine had run out. Mary, Jesus' mother, told Him about the problem.

Close by were six stone water jars that could hold somewhere between twenty to thirty gallons. Jesus told the servants to fill all the jars with water. Jesus turned this water into wine! One of the servants took some of the new wine to the master of the banquet to try, and he was amazed. He said it was the best wine he had ever tasted. The Bible says that this was the first sign that Jesus did to reveal His glory.

The next miracle Jesus performed involved healing an official's son. (You can find this story in John 4:46–54.) This miracle also happened in Cana, because the official had heard that Jesus was there and went to see Him. The sick boy was in a distant town called Capernaum. When the boy's father found Jesus, he begged Jesus to come back with him to their home and heal the boy.

Jesus told the man to go home because his son would live. The Bible says that the man believed Jesus and went home. The man's servants met him on the road before he reached his house with the wonderful news that the boy was indeed alive. When the father asked what time the boy got better, the servants said it was the exact same time that Jesus had said the boy would live! The official's entire household believed in Jesus because of this amazing miracle!

Another great miracle Jesus performed was in Capernaum when He went to the home of His friend Peter's mother-in-law. She was very sick and had a very high fever (Luke 4:38–39). Jesus got close to the woman and commanded the fever to go away. And just like that, the woman was well. That's how powerful Jesus is!

That evening at sunset, people brought others who had all kinds of sickness to Jesus in hopes that He would heal them. Jesus loved them all and laid His hands on them and healed them.

In Luke 5:3–10, we find another miracle of Jesus that involved a ton of fish. Jesus was on a boat talking to people on the shore, and then He told Peter to take the boat farther out on the lake. Jesus told Peter to let down the fishing nets so they could catch some fish. Peter told Jesus that they had already worked hard at fishing all night and didn't catch one single fish. However, Peter said that because it was Jesus who gave the order, he would obey. When Peter did what the Lord had told him, the fishermen caught so many fish that their nets began to break! Then Peter asked for help from his friends who were in another boat. There were so many fish that both boats began to sink!

Peter knelt down before Jesus and told Him to go away because he was a sinner. Jesus told Peter not to be afraid and that from that point on, he would be a fisher of men.

In Luke 5:12–15, we find another miracle where Jesus healed a man

CLUES

In John 15, Jesus provides a beautiful picture of how He blesses His followers and how life is meant to be lived. Jesus says that He is the Vine and we are the branches. When we stay connected to Him, we thrive. If we break away from Him, then we lose out on all the things He has for us.

who had a terrible skin disease called leprosy. The man saw Jesus and fell to the ground. He said that if Jesus was willing to heal him, then he knew the disease would leave his body. Jesus told the man that He wanted to help and said, "Be clean!" (v. 13). At that very moment, the man was healed.

Then there was the time, recorded in Matthew 8:5–13, when a Roman soldier sent helpers to ask Jesus for a favor. The centurion's servant was so sick that he was about to die. Jesus said He would go to the house and heal the servant. The interesting thing is that the centurion didn't feel worthy to have Jesus come to his house. But he had faith in Jesus, for he told Jesus just to say the word and he knew his servant would be healed. The Bible says that Jesus was amazed at the man's faith and healed the servant from a distance.

Another time, Jesus was staying in a house and a large crowd had gathered inside and outside.

There was a group of men who had a friend who was paralyzed. They wanted to bring the man to Jesus, but they couldn't get him in the house because there was such a large crowd of people. So the friends carried the paralyzed man up to the roof of the house and lowered him down inside. They placed him right in front of Jesus. When Jesus saw the faith of the man's friends, He told

the paralyzed man that his sins were forgiven.

 **CLUES**

This miraculous healing is important because it shows that Jesus really is the Son of God.

Then Jesus told the man to get up and go home. And he did!

The man immediately got up and began praising God for the miracle and a second chance at life. All the people were amazed at what Jesus had just done for the paralyzed man. They too began to praise God for the awesome healing they had witnessed (Luke 5:18–26).

Another time Jesus was in the synagogue on the Sabbath, and a man with a deformed hand was there too. Jesus told the man to stand up in front of everyone so that He could teach the people a lesson. The Pharisees didn't believe Jesus was the Savior, and they tried to accuse Him of doing wrong things. They didn't think it was right to heal anyone on the Sabbath. Jesus told the man to stretch out his hand, and as soon as he did, the man's hand was healed. Jesus was trying to get the people to see that to do good and help others is the right way to live, no matter the day of the week (Mark 3:1–6).

Once, Jesus and His friends were traveling to a city called Nain. When they arrived at the town gate, they saw a child who had died. Jesus miraculously brought the child back to life. The boy was his mother's only child. Jesus told her not to cry because He had compassion on her. Some people in the crowd said, "God has come to help his people" (Luke 7:16).

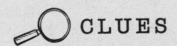

CLUES

This miracle shows us just how amazing the power of Jesus really is. Jesus speaks and lives change.

Yet another time, Jesus had the opportunity to show His disciples that everything

is under God's control. They were out on a lake
when a bad storm came over them. Jesus was
sleeping in the boat while the waves grew and
the winds roared. The men were scared that the
storm would be deadly, so they wakened Jesus for
His help. When Jesus woke, He asked His friends

why their faith in Him was so weak. Then Jesus got up and spoke directly to the storm, and the weather immediately improved. The disciples were amazed that even the wind and water obey Jesus (Matthew 8:23–27).

One day a man named Jairus came to Jesus because his only daughter was dying. Jesus headed to the man's house to help the girl, but He was stopped on the way to heal a woman who was also suffering. By the time Jesus reached Jairus's home, He discovered that the girl had already died. "Don't be afraid," Jesus said. "Just believe, and she will be healed." Jesus entered the home and held the girl. Immediately she came back to life (Luke 8:41–42, 49–56).

One of the greatest expressions of Jesus' love for people came when He performed a miracle that involved food. The Bible says that a large crowd had gathered to hear Jesus speak, but they were very hungry. A boy had five small loaves of bread and two fish in his lunch. Jesus told the people to sit down. Then He gave thanks for the provision, and His friends started handing out bread to everyone present. Jesus did the same with the fish. Five thousand men and their

families were fed that afternoon. And not only that, but when everyone was done eating, Jesus had His friends collect twelve basketfuls of the leftover bread (John 6:5–14)!

After the massive hillside meal, Jesus went off by Himself to pray. He sent the disciples ahead of Him, telling them to go by boat. After some time had passed, Jesus saw that His friends' boat was caught in a small storm. Jesus performed another miracle by walking on water to help His friends. At first His friends were afraid, but as soon as Jesus climbed into the boat with them, the wind died down. At that point, the disciples worshipped Jesus, calling Him the Son of God (Matthew 14:22-32).

CLUES

Scripture records many more miracles that Jesus performed. These examples show how all of creation obeys Jesus. He truly is Lord of all!

Prayer

Jesus prayed often. His disciples even asked Him to teach them how to pray. One time Jesus went to a mountain and prayed all night. Jesus asked His disciples to pray for people who would be willing to go out and share the gospel. There were times that Jesus would pray in thanksgiving, and other times He would pray for people to believe that He was the Son of God. Jesus wanted to set the example for us to pray without giving up.

Jesus told us to pray. Prayer was not something Jesus did to cross off a spiritual home-work list; it was a much-needed path to approach God. Jesus

 CLUES

God answers our prayers, and reading our Bibles will help us find answers.

taught us to ask, seek, and knock when it comes to prayer. He said that when we ask we will receive, when we seek we will find, and when we knock doors will open.

Jesus also taught people to pray and to have faith that God is who He says He is. Jesus told us not to doubt and also that we are to forgive people so we have nothing holding us back as we approach God with our requests.

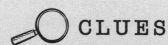 **CLUES**

Prayer is our chance to talk to our heavenly Father. Jesus gave us a model prayer called the Lord's Prayer found in Matthew 6:9–13. This prayer helps us understand our position as a child of God. He is our Father, and we know we are loved by Him, so our natural reaction should be to use our prayer as a way of thanking Him for all He has done for us.

Jesus taught us to be humble and to constantly ask God to be merciful to us.

Before Jesus took up His cross, He prayed. This is when He was very sad and asked God to

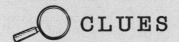

CLUES

As we pray, we need to remember that God always wants what's best for us. The important thing to know is that Jesus understands what we are going through. He loves us so much that He gave up His life so that we could be forgiven. That alone should cause our prayers to be full of praise and thanksgiving.

take away the upcoming ordeal of the cross. But Jesus immediately prayed for God's will to be done (Matthew 26:39–42).

Jesus also modeled praying before meals. He prayed prayers of thanksgiving during the last meal He shared with His friends before His crucifixion (Mark 14:22), two times when He miraculously fed thousands of people (Mark 6:41 and 8:6), and again after He rose from the dead and shared a meal with a few of his followers in Emmaus (Luke 24:30). Jesus used these events to teach us that our hearts should be grateful to God for every blessing that He chooses to give us.

Jesus made prayer a natural part of His day. Whether He was sitting down for a meal or out walking with His friends, He always made time to pray. Jesus knew how important it was to talk to God, and we will be blessed to remember this truth.

 **CLUES**

Prayer helps us to connect with God, and it should encourage us to know that even when we forget to pray or don't know what to pray, Jesus is always there for us. In the New Testament book of Hebrews, we find a verse that reminds us not to worry when it comes to faltering in our prayer life. In Hebrews 7:25, we read that Jesus always intercedes for us. That means even now, Jesus is covering our lives in prayer!

We don't need to limit our praying to before school and before bed. Find times during the day to tell God how you're feeling and to praise Him for all the things He has

done for you. Let your prayer time be a natural

part of your day, and be grateful for how God will

work in your life and

help you do great

things for His glory!

 **CLUES**

In Matthew 6:5–6, Jesus said, "Do not be like the hypocrites. . .standing in the synagogues and on the street corners to be seen by others. . . . Go into your room, close the door and pray to your Father, who is unseen." Of course, you can pray anywhere, at any time. Jesus was trying to get us to see that the second example is more personal when it's just us and God.

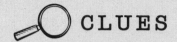# CLUES

Jesus wants His children to be joyful. He wants our prayers to bring us joy to the fullest (John 16:23–27). This should guide us to the place where our prayers give us the courage and boldness to minister to those around us. Jesus prayed, but He also acted. We need to follow His example and be a blessing to others. And, as we are being a blessing, we are called to be like Jesus and pray with others (Luke 9:28).

5

The Final Days

The last week that Jesus was on earth, many things happened that will help you to get a bigger picture of our Lord. To start, Jesus was spending time with a family in the town of Bethany. While He was there, a woman came carrying a jar filled with very expensive perfume. As Jesus was sitting at a table, the woman poured the perfume on His head. The disciples were angry because they thought the perfume could be sold and the money given to the poor.

Jesus corrected His friends and told them that the woman did a beautiful thing. He told them that we will always have the poor to serve but that He was about to leave them. Jesus said the woman was anointing Him and preparing Him for burial.

While this event took place, back in Jerusalem one of the disciples named Judas Iscariot made plans to betray Jesus. The chief priests gave Judas thirty pieces of silver, so he agreed to look for an opportunity to hand Jesus over to them.

Soon after, Jesus had the Last Supper with all His friends. He knew that Judas had made plans to turn Him over to the officials. He told His friends that one of them would betray Him, and

Judas asked Jesus if He meant him. Jesus said, "You have said so" (Matthew 26:25).

As they ate, Jesus took the bread and gave thanks. He broke it and said that the bread represented His body. And after they all ate the bread, Jesus took a cup of wine and again gave thanks for it. Jesus said, "Drink from it, all of you. This is my blood of the covenant, which is poured out

for many for the forgiveness of sins" (Matthew 26:27–28). Jesus was saying that soon, when He was hanging on the cross, He would be dying for the world's sins.

After dinner, Jesus and His friends sang a hymn and went to the Mount of Olives. At that point, Jesus predicted that His friend Peter would deny, or disown, Him—not once but three times. Peter said He would never do that to Jesus.

Then Jesus went to the garden called Gethsemane to pray. Jesus was overwhelmed with sorrow and asked His friends to keep watch while He was praying. Jesus then prayed to God and asked "if it is possible, may this cup be taken from me. Yet not as I will, but as you will" (Matthew 26:39). Jesus knew that the time had come for Him to be handed over to be crucified. When Jesus returned to His disciples, He found them sleeping. He told them to keep watch as He went away a second time to pray.

Jesus prayed again and asked God if there was a way that He could avoid the upcoming sacrifice.

But for a second time, He said that He wanted God's will to be done. And again, when Jesus went back, He found His disciples sleeping. He told them to get up because He knew He was about to be betrayed.

As Jesus was saying these things, Judas arrived along with a crowd of men armed with swords and clubs. Judas walked up to Jesus and kissed Him. This was a sign to the guards that Jesus was the man they needed to arrest. One of the disciples grabbed a sword and tried to defend Jesus, but Jesus told Him to put the sword away. Jesus said if He needed protection, He could call on God to send "more than twelve legions of angels" to help (Matthew 26:53). Jesus went on to say that these things had to happen in order for the scriptures to be fulfilled. And, at that point, the Bible says that all of the disciples abandoned Jesus and fled.

Jesus was brought before a group of people known as the Sanhedrin. They were the elders and chief priests, like the Supreme Court of their day. They were trying to find enough evidence to put Jesus to death because they didn't think He was the Messiah. But they couldn't find any proof. The men finally asked Jesus if He was the Son of God, and Jesus replied that He was.

The priests were angry because they didn't believe Jesus and thought He was being blasphemous. They thought He was making fun of God. Then a very sad thing happened. The people spit on Jesus and hit Him.

During this time, Peter was out in the courtyard

when a girl came up to him. She said that she knew Peter was with Jesus. Peter quickly said that he didn't know what she was talking about. Peter left and went to the gateway where another girl saw him and said that Peter was a friend of Jesus. And again he said, "I don't know the man!" (Matthew 26:72). Finally, more people approached Peter and said that he was with Jesus. Peter got angry and again said that he didn't know Jesus. Then, just as Jesus had predicted, a rooster crowed, and Peter remembered that he said he wouldn't deny his friend. Peter ran away and cried.

The leaders tied Jesus up and handed Him over to a man named Pontius Pilate, the governor. Pilate questioned Jesus, asking Him if He was the King of the Jews. Jesus replied, "You have said so" (Matthew 27:11). Then all the chief priests started accusing Jesus, but He remained silent. So the governor decided to follow his custom of releasing a prisoner chosen by the crowd. There was a well-known prisoner named Barabbas, and Pilate asked the people who they wanted to set free: "Jesus who is called the Messiah" (Matthew 27:17) or Barabbas.

At this point, Pilate's wife came to him and said this about Jesus: "Don't have anything to do with that innocent man, for I have suffered a great deal today in a dream because of him" (Matthew 27:19). Pilate didn't listen to his wife and asked the crowd a second time who they wanted to release. And the answer was Barabbas. Pilate then asked the crowd what he should do with Jesus, and they yelled, "Crucify him!" (Matthew 27:22).

Pilate then washed his hands in front of the crowd, saying that he wasn't responsible for what was happening to Jesus. He released Barabbas and had Jesus flogged and then handed Him over to be crucified. The Roman soldiers stripped Jesus and put a red robe on Him. They made a crown of thorns and set it on His head and put a staff in His right hand. They were making fun of Jesus. It was very sad. When they were finished mocking him, they took the robe off Jesus and put His own clothes back on Him, then led Him away to be crucified.

Jesus carried His cross to a hill outside of Jerusalem called Golgotha. He was crucified on a cross between two criminals. Even while Jesus hung on the cross, people still insulted Him. They

said that if He was the Messiah, then He could save Himself or even have God save Him. For three hours in the middle of the day the sky was dark. After many hours on the cross, Jesus cried out and "gave up his spirit" (Matthew 27:50).

At that very moment, the temple curtain was torn in two, the earth rumbled, rocks split in half, and many people were raised to life. This means that they were dead before Jesus was on the cross, but when Jesus died their bodies were brought back to life!

The guards who had been making fun of Jesus then proclaimed that Jesus was the Son of God. A man named Joseph of Arimathea went to the governor and asked for Jesus' body. He wrapped it in clean linen and placed Jesus in a new tomb. A large stone was rolled in front of the entrance.

The chief priests went to Pilate and asked that he have a guard watch the tomb of Jesus because they remembered Jesus had said that after three days, He would rise again. They were afraid that

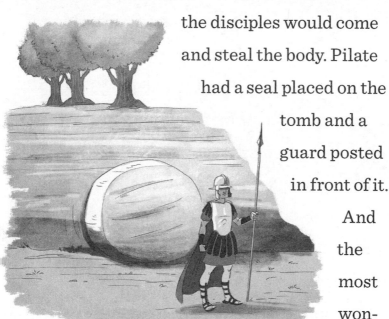

the disciples would come and steal the body. Pilate had a seal placed on the tomb and a guard posted in front of it. And the most won-derful

part of the whole story is that on the third day, just as He said He would, Jesus conquered death and rose from the grave! He appeared to all His friends and instructed them to go out and make new disciples in all the nations and baptize them and teach them all the things Jesus had taught them.

Finally, Jesus told His disciples that He would be with them forever.

Jesus appeared to many people after His resurrection. One of His friends, Thomas, didn't believe that Jesus had actually come back from the grave. Jesus didn't judge Thomas. He simply appeared to His friend so that He would believe the truth.

Jesus appeared to His friends at least three times after His resurrection. In the gospel of John, we read that Jesus prepared a breakfast to share with them. The end of the gospel says that Jesus did many other things with his friends. The book of Acts says that Jesus was with His friends

for forty days "and spoke about the kingdom of God" (1:3). Jesus told His friends to wait for the gift of the Holy Spirit. And then the Bible says that Jesus was taken up to heaven and "a cloud hid him from their sight" (1:9).

When we read Acts 9, we see that Jesus appeared to a man named Saul. Saul had been making bad choices, trying to threaten the Lord's disciples. One day Saul was riding on his horse to the town of Damascus when a light from heaven exploded all around him. Saul then heard Jesus speak to him: "Saul, Saul, why do you persecute me?" When Saul asked who was speaking, Jesus said, "I am Jesus, whom you are persecuting" (Acts 9:4–5). Saul was temporarily blinded. Later on, he had his sight restored by a man named Ananias, and Saul would eventually change his name to Paul. Paul would spend the rest of his life telling people about Jesus!

Names of Jesus

One of the most interesting things about Jesus is that He has many names. And from those names we learn so much about His heart and character. Here's a list of just a few of the names of Jesus:

- Immanuel—God with us (Matthew 1:23). What a comfort to know that Jesus is always by our side. We never have to worry that our God has gone away in search of someone else to have a relationship with. Jesus thinks so much about you that He left His throne in heaven to come down to earth and become your sacrifice.

- The Everlasting God (Isaiah 40:28). If you have asked Jesus to be the Lord of your life and have asked Him to forgive your sins, then you will be with Him forever. What a blessing!

- God my Savior (Luke 1:47)
- The Most High (Luke 1:76). Jesus is more important and above all things in this life. His life testified to His position as Savior.

CLUES

All of these names point to the truth that Jesus goes with you. He lifts you up and understands your heartaches. He understands your bad days. Jesus is there to carry your burdens and to help you get through your day.

- The True God (1 John 5:20). The fact that Jesus is true means you can trust Him and follow His lead.
- Wonderful Counselor (Isaiah 9:6). He is our wonderful gift, and we should treasure the fact that His love for us never ends.
- Beloved Son (Matthew 17:5)
- God in the flesh (1 Timothy 3:16)

- King of glory (Psalm 24:8)
- The Lord Our Righteous Savior (Jeremiah 23:6). This name gives us confidence that the One who took our place on the cross is worthy of our worship.
- Son of Man (John 8:28)
- Alpha and Omega (Revelation 1:8)
- Sustainer of all things (Hebrews 1:3)
- The Way and the Truth and the Life (John 14:6)
- God's Righteous Servant (Isaiah 53:11)
- Great Prophet (Luke 7:16)

 CLUES

Pause for a moment and consider how Jesus is personally reaching out to you. Think about each one of His names and picture Jesus being that for you. Pray that He lights your path as you struggle to make a hard decision. Ask Him to watch over you as a shepherd watches his sheep. Stay plugged in to Jesus and know He is your source of everything.

- A Man of Suffering (Isaiah 53:3)
- Savior of the world (1 John 4:14)
- Messiah (John 4:25)
- Lamb of God (John 1:29)
- Good Shepherd (John 10:11)
- Vine (John 15:5)
- Bread of Life (John 6:35)
- True Light (John 1:9)
- Light of the world (John 8:12)
- A Refuge for the needy; a Shelter from the storm (Isaiah 25:4)
- Refuge for His people (Joel 3:16)
- Rock Eternal (Isaiah 26:4)
- Foundation (1 Corinthians 3:11)
- Precious Cornerstone (1 Peter 2:6)
- Holy Place (Isaiah 8:14)
- Great High Priest (Hebrews 4:14)
- Redeemer (Isaiah 59:20)
- Truth (John 14:6)

- Holy One (Acts 2:27)
- Pioneer and Perfecter of faith (Hebrews 12:2)
- Deliverer (Romans 11:26)
- Shield (Psalm 84:9)
- Lord of lords; King of kings (Revelation 17:14)
- Lord of All (Acts 10:36)
- Prince of Peace (Isaiah 9:6)
- Hope (1 Timothy 1:1)
- Portion (Jeremiah 10:16)
- Helper (Hebrews 13:6)
- Healer (Luke 9:11)
- Example (John 13:15)
- Resting Place (Jeremiah 50:6)
- All in All (Colossians 3:11)

7

Now that we've investigated the life of Jesus, we have great lessons we can learn from Him. From His humble birth in a manger to His dramatic death and resurrection, Jesus did a lot of great kingdom work for the glory of His heavenly Father. If you haven't done so already, considering all the facts in this book and praying for Jesus to give you new life is a great idea.

Let's look at each one of these valuable lessons individually along with some memory verses that will help plant God's truth in our hearts. Then we will be equipped with power to do the work God has called us to do. God is ready to use you at your young age to do great things!

Power-Up # 1:

JESUS IS THE

ONLY ANSWER.

Many things in our lives will compete for our attention. Jesus is the only thing that matters. Living for Him is the best way to live.

MEMORY VERSE: "I am the way and the truth and the life. No one comes to the Father except through me."

JOHN 14:6

Power-Up #2:
READ YOUR BIBLE.

We need to make a habit of reading God's Word, knowing that it will help us understand what God desires and will give us a bigger picture of what He wants specifically for us. Then we can be ready to be used by the Father to do kingdom work for His glory.

MEMORY VERSE: Man does not live on bread alone but on every word that comes from the mouth of the LORD.

DEUTERONOMY 8:3

Power-Up #3:

WORSHIP GOD.

Jesus spent His earthly ministry worshipping His heavenly Father. His life was an example for us to follow. We can worship God every day through our words and actions, especially in the way we treat others.

MEMORY VERSE: Therefore, I urge you, brothers and sisters, in view of God's mercy, to offer your bodies as a living sacrifice, holy and pleasing to God—this is your true and proper worship.

ROMANS 12:1

Power-Up #4:

LOVE THE LOST.

It doesn't matter how young or old we are. Jesus set an example for us to love other people like He loves us. This includes having a heart for those people who might not know Jesus. Telling them about Jesus and praying for them is a great way to be like Jesus.

MEMORY VERSE: "For the Son of Man came to seek and to save the lost."
LUKE 19:10

Power-Up #5:
JUST BELIEVE.

We have an enemy who tries to distract us from our walk with Jesus. This is the same enemy who tried to tempt Jesus in the desert. When we read our Bibles and believe that Jesus is our Savior, we can have courage because we know that Jesus protects us and will never let us go.

MEMORY VERSE: "Don't be afraid; just believe." MARK 5:36

Power-Up #6:

SHOW MERCY.

Showing mercy means that we really think about other people and their feelings. Treating others with respect and kindness is being merciful because that lets them know that they are important and that they matter to God.

MEMORY VERSE: "Be merciful, just as your Father is merciful." LUKE 6:36

Power-Up #7:
EXTEND GRACE.

When someone makes you mad because they've hurt your feelings, you might be tempted to respond in anger. But showing grace means showing them a better way. It means showing them Jesus. Giving grace means responding in love, because that's how Jesus responds to us.

MEMORY VERSE: We have seen his glory, the glory of the one and only Son, who came from the Father, full of grace and truth. JOHN 1:14

Power-Up #8:
FORGIVE.

Forgiving someone is never easy. But it was very important to Jesus, so it has to be important to us as we go about our kingdom work of telling people about Him. Forgiving someone doesn't mean you are weak; it means that you are obeying Jesus.

MEMORY VERSE: Then Peter came to Jesus and asked, "Lord, how many times shall I forgive my brother or sister who sins against me? Up to seven times?" Jesus answered, "I tell you, not seven times, but seventy-seven times."
Matthew 18:21-22

Power-Up #9:

BE JOYFUL.

Jesus wants us to be full of joy. This happens when we realize how blessed we are to be called children of God. Know that Jesus is with you every day and that He helps you get through every situation, good or bad. Find joy in the fact that He loves you very much and has great plans for your life.

MEMORY VERSE: "I have told you this so that my joy may be in you and that your joy may be complete." JOHN 15:11

Power-Up #10:
PRAY.

Talking to God and telling Him what's on your heart is just what Jesus did. He made it a habit to pray and talk to God about everything. Making prayer a habit will help us stay connected to Jesus. He hears every word we speak and is there to help us no matter what we're going through.

MEMORY VERSE: "God has heard your prayer." Acts 10:31

IMAGINE. . .

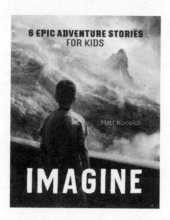

For the first time since its release, the Imagine series is available with all 6 titles under one cover!

You'll join boys and girls—just like you!—who find themselves back in Bible times, living out epic adventures.

Stories include:
Imagine. . .The Great Flood
Imagine. . .The Ten Plagues
Imagine. . .The Fall of Jericho
Imagine. . .The Giant's Fall
Imagine. . .The Miracles of Jesus
Imagine. . .The Tower Rising

Paperback / 978-1-63609-197-6/ $14.99